Sex, Nursery
& Other ~~~

BOOKS BY DR. PETER MARSHALL

Now I Know Why Tigers Eat Their Young:
How to Survive Your Teenagers with Humor

Cinderella Revisited: How to Survive Your
Stepfamily Without a Fairy Godmother

Sex, Nursery Rhymes & Other Evils

A LOOK AT THE BIZARRE,
AMUSING, SOMETIMES SHOCKING ADVICE
OF VICTORIAN CHILDCARE EXPERTS

by Dr. Peter Marshall

WHITECAP BOOKS
Vancouver / Toronto

The information in this book is true and complete to the best of
our knowledge. All recommendations are made without guarantee on the
part of the author or Whitecap Books Ltd. The author and publisher disclaim
any liability in connection with the use of this information. For
additional information please contact Whitecap Books Ltd.,
351 Lynn Avenue, North Vancouver, BC V7J 2C4.

Edited by Elaine Jones
Cover design by Rose Cowles
Book design by Stephen Gregory
Typeset by SKMB Communication by Design
Printed and bound in Canada.

CANADIAN CATALOGUING IN PUBLICATION DATA
Marshall, Peter Graham, 1947–
Sex, nursery rhymes and other evils
Includes bibliographical references and index.
ISBN 1-55110-252-8
1. Child-rearing – History. 2. Parenting. 3. Parent and child.
I. Title
HQ769.M37 1994   649'.1'09034   C94-910421-3

Kathy, this one is just for you, with love.

ACKNOWLEDGMENTS

My thanks to Corley Knowles for her help locating material for the book. I am also indebted to Professor Snell at the University of Guelph who so generously took the time to provide a list of references, all of which proved very valuable. Mary-Jayne VanPypen survived the final and most demanding stages of preparing the manuscript and somehow managed to retain her composure in spite of all the unreasonable demands associated with deadlines that were either imminent or passing. Thank you.

CONTENTS

CONTENTS

Preface

THERE IS something unique about the job of being a parent. Somehow it remains extremely popular in spite of the fact that it offers no pay, no promotions, and no thanks. In a desperate effort to gain at least some appreciation we have created Mother's Day and Father's Day. I suppose one day off each year is a beginning, but we're not exactly a tribute to the labor movement.

The job is also very demanding and requires a great deal of skill. We begin with the responsibility for an infant who is totally dependent on us. We are supposed to know what she needs and how to provide it, even though she has very limited ways of communicating. We end up with the responsibility for a teenager who insists she is dependent on us for nothing, but who is saving us from loneliness by continuing to grace us with her presence. We are supposed to know how to make the experience successful and to live with the fact that she has far too many ways of communicating exactly what she thinks, feels, and wants.

My own career as a parent began twenty-eight years ago. Why I still have a house full of children as young as five is a question that keeps me awake at nights and bewilders those of my friends who are already enjoying the empty-nest syndrome. I like to tell my children that the reason for having a large family was the hope that sooner or later one would turn out right, but they fail to find this even faintly amusing.

While being a parent has been a major part of almost all my adult life, I received no training for the job. On the few occasions when I have time to engage in reflection, I wonder why I adopted a particular approach to raising my children. I also wonder why it has changed so much over the last three decades; l certainly cannot claim to have been consistent when it comes to child-rearing. My debut was as a twenty-year-old in the sixties and our family life was based on the belief that freedom of expression was all that was needed for children to grow in an atmosphere of peace and harmony. My first two, Joanne and Tim, called me by my first name and were enrolled in a free school. Somehow they survived in spite of the fact that they spent their early years in a single-parent home that was part hovel, part commune and surrounded by a cast of characters who were determined to suppress any potential they might have had to become pillars of middle-class society. Fortunately, none was adopted as a role model, and although structure, routines, and orderliness remained foreign concepts in our household until the children were preteens, they managed to reach adulthood intact. By the time the next child was born I was considerably older and, while not necessarily wiser, was married to someone who never had so much as an inkling to write poetry or put flowers in her hair. Kathy and I are raising Aaron, Kiera, and Alexandra very differently. They call me "dad" and I would happily agree to "sir," they attend regular schools, their daily lives are predictable, and their clothes match. The search for domestic peace and harmony continues, but I am now willing to accept that a reasonable substitute can be procured through use of prolonged banishment to their rooms or, better still, a lengthy stay with a kindly and unsuspecting relative.

The changes in child-rearing style that have occurred in my own history as a parent do not necessarily represent improvements. Although I would not want to return to my earlier way of life, this is not only because I want to stay married to Kathy. It also reflects the fact that, as a parent in my late forties, I am a very different person than I was in my twenties. A similar lack of consistency can be found when I compare our current views and practices to those of our friends and relatives. Aaron holds a record for the length of time a green vegetable has not passed his lips and would tremble at the thought of trading places with his cousin who has to finish *everything*, including Brussels sprouts. At five, Alexandra is permitted to go on sleep-overs (encouraged to go would be more accurate), but has a friend whose parents do not feel this type of separation is a good idea at such a young age. Some of us are highly selective when it comes to the movies and television programs our children watch; others rarely act as censors. We do not always share the same views regarding discipline, and while some of their friends are quite adept at budgeting, our children have yet to receive a regular allowance.

For many years I have taken the position that the vast differences in child-rearing styles are not, of themselves, a problem. If there were a single recipe for successful parenting it could be argued that we should all try to conform to the *one* tried and true method. Such a recipe does not exist and parents must develop their own policies and procedures manual. If we have been fortunate, our own experiences as children will have provided a thorough training ground. We do not, of course, use our personal histories as the only guide. On occasions we will actively seek *not* to emulate the child-rearing practices of our own parents. Sometimes we will be successful in coming up with alternative approaches; sometimes we will not, and contrary to our determination to be different, old patterns will reemerge. I remember vowing never to expose my children to repetitive lectures; I was given many in my youth because of my tendency to collect rather than overcome faults. But the temptation to use my offsprings' failings as a cue to sharing the vast expanses of my wisdom is irresistible. So far they have hidden their admiration and gratitude behind a facade of scorn and indifference, but I am not deterred. Another solemn oath was never, never to begin a sentence with, "When I was your age . . ."; I lied.

The first serious attack on my belief that, like most parents, I can usually manage to survive without damaging my children irreparably came when I was browsing through the childcare section of a second-hand bookstore. The more I read, the more I began to experience an overwhelming feeling of guilt. Not only had my years as a parent been characterized by ignorance and ineptitude, I had been nothing short of unfit. At that very moment Aaron could have been at home playing marbles or solitaire. How could I have ever let him engage in activities that posed such a threat to his moral well-being? Why had we allowed the girls to take math? Did we not know that math in general, and geometry in particular, placed them at risk for infertility? And could we ever be forgiven for allowing them to have sugared cereal for breakfast? In one fell swoop they had been propelled towards a life of drunkenness and debauchery.

You will not be alone if you too were unaware of the dangers described above. All of the books had been published in the Victorian era and it is unlikely that the views and opinions they contained would ever come to your attention. At first this interest in Victorian childcare literature stemmed from the fact that I needed to complete a degree and the choice of writing a paper on the history of the family was a welcomed change from yet another project on how to get dogs to salivate or rats to traverse mazes. This interest was sustained, however, by the discovery that so much of the advice given to Victorian parents was amusing, bizarre, and even shocking when viewed from a late-twentieth-century perspective. As I read on, I also began to appreciate the relevance of this period in history for parents and professionals alike. Experts have been eager to market their ideas on the assumption that there *is* a recipe for successful parenting and they have heaped scorn on the notion that we can view our personal experiences and ingenuity as our chief assets. But how "expert" have the experts been and what has entitled them to speak with authority? Have their theories been sound and have they produced the evidence to justify the advice they offer so freely to parents? Assuming that some of their ideas were mistaken, how damaging were their errors? These questions became the starting point of this book. Chapter by chapter it examines various aspects of child-rearing. While I hope the contents will often be humorous and entertaining, I have indulged myself with yet further brief moments of reflection on the issues faced by all parents, past and present.

1. The Advice Industry

I DOUBT THAT there has ever been a shortage of people willing to advise others on how to raise their offspring. Senior family members often provide this service free of charge. (I vow not to do this to my children – this time I really mean it.) On other occasions the advice will be sought and the willingness of parents to listen to other people's ideas and suggestions has helped to keep generations of childcare specialists in work. These experts have become increasingly common and are found in many professions including medicine, nursing, social work, and psychology. They are employed in numerous agencies and run private practices specializing in child and family counseling. They also publish the many books that can be found in the childcare sections of libraries and bookstores and they contribute to the growing number of magazines devoted to parenting. Experts appear regularly on television and radio talk shows and they offer courses and workshops on topics ranging from prenatal care to surviving the teenage years.

The growth of the advice-giving industry is in keeping with the notion of the Information Age. Data, facts, and opinions are so easy to obtain and transmit. Home-computer technology already permits rapid access to vast amounts of material, and within my lifetime the contents of an entire library should be available for electronic storage and use in the home.

Back in Their Day

The advice industry is not, however, a recent phenomenon; its growth and status were achieved primarily during the last century. By the time of the future Queen of England's birth in 1819, the industrial revolution was bringing about far-reaching changes in the Western world. Both North America and Europe were experiencing a major restructuring of their societies. Economies that had been primarily agrarian became increasingly industrial and commercial. The population distribution shifted accordingly, with more and more families being concentrated in urban areas. The distinction between male and female roles became more rigid; the husband was employed outside the home, while the wife's world was almost exclusively domestic.

Industrialization also led to major changes in the philosophy and practice of education. In early Victorian times schools did not have the prominent position they occupy today. As the century progressed, however, emphasis needed to be placed on ensuring that the future generation would have the knowledge and expertise required to maintain a competitive edge in industry and technology. Education became essential; it also became more specialized and was offered through a rapidly growing system of public schooling that was to become compulsory. As the century drew to a close, childhood became a lengthy training period during which the responsibility for producing competitive members of society was shared between school and home.

Prolonging the period of education and dependency was also in keeping with a more general shift in the attitudes towards childhood. Prior to the Victorian era children were often seen as mini-adults and the parents' task was to make sure they acted accordingly as soon as possible. This way of thinking was eroded, however, by the growing number of writers who subscribed to the view that childhood was a qualitatively distinct period of development consisting of a number of different stages. By implication, children did not have the same needs as adults. Because they could not be understood or managed by applying the principles that operated in the adult world, a separate body of knowledge was needed.

Rapid change inevitably brings a measure of uncertainty and insecurity. It was no longer sufficient to rely on the old ways and base child-rearing on the wisdom and practice of the previous generation. A new model or blueprint of family life was emerging and this created the ideal climate for the advice industry to prosper. Childcare experts were there to guide, direct, and instruct. They became established as professionals and scientists and, in this respect, they benefited from the rapid growth of scientific theories and research that took place in the Victorian era. The advances made in fields such as medicine and physics led to a greater acceptance of the idea that the laws governing nature could, in principle, be discovered. God still ruled supreme, but His universe did not have to remain so mysterious. It followed that children's development and behavior should also be lawful and experts were, therefore, needed to discover the cause-and-effect relationships that could form the basis for successful parenting. Psychology departments and child research laboratories appeared in a number of universities and the new disciplines of pediatrics and child psychiatry were gaining influence and status.

This new-found status afforded the experts considerable power; whenever I am confronted with the advice of someone I respect, I have to deal with the guilt that arises from the fact that I am probably not following it. The Victorian experts not only induced such guilt, they also threw caution to the wind in asserting that those parents who ignored their prescriptions would have no one but themselves to blame when the lives of their offspring and even their descendants were irrevocably harmed.

By the time Victoria died in 1901, the experts had acquired a level of power that ensured their tenure. Their books were received with enthusiasm and many writers of this era reached heights of popularity that would be the envy of most modern-day authors. The advice industry had boomed and all aspects of childcare were scrutinized. Whether it was a major topic, such as education or sexuality, or a specific issue, such as the impact of wearing slippers or riding a bicycle, there was a wealth of opinion to be found. Some of the advice was dismissed or forgotten long before our generation became parents. No one today is cautioned not to allow books of nursery rhymes into the house for fear that the child's growth will be stunted, and I doubt that too many people even know that such a concern ever existed. In other areas, however, the advice has remained influential. Debates regarding breast-feeding or the significance of bed-wetting, the prevalence of anxiety regarding masturbation, and even the popularity of breakfast cereals are all part of the legacy from the Victorian childcare experts.

2. Spare the Rod

IT IS HARD to be indifferent to how our offspring behave. We know that other parents, like ourselves, rate children on a scale with "Oh, she's so polite and well behaved" at one end, to "I hate to say it, but she's such a little brat" at the other. We encourage our children to associate with those we have placed at the former end and hope they will not descend to the depths of the latter – at least not in public.

How to manage and control children is an issue that has been discussed by many generations of childcare experts and entire books have been devoted to the topic of discipline. The implicit assumption is that children cannot be left to their own devices; they need us to provide limits and direction.

Although discipline is typically seen as part of the business of being a parent, the details of this part of the job description have varied. So much depends on how children are perceived. Are they basically pleasant creatures who need a gentle nudge now and then, or are they like wild beasts who need to be subdued and trained before being let loose on society? You also have to decide what standards to set for their behavior. What can you expect from a child and at what age do you apply the same standards as operate in the adult world? How these questions should be answered became a topic of much debate in the Victorian era and had far-reaching implications for child-rearing practices.

Little Devils?

I was buying a card the other day for a friend who had just had a baby. The experience of browsing through the large display was a powerful reminder of the positive attitude we have towards infants. The new arrivals were compared to angels, rainbows encircled their heads, and songbirds fluttered about their cradles. The messages reminded parents of the happiness and bliss that were now theirs and none even hinted at the research indicating that babies, however welcome, are a significant source of stress on families, particularly during the first year: there is a good reason why social scientists don't get to write for greeting-card companies.

There was a time when such cards would have been considered ludicrous. Prior to the Victorian era there was a strong belief that infants were innately bad; it was as if they had almost cornered the market on original sin. There is an account of a minister who warned parents that, "as innocent as children seem to be, they are young vipers. They are infinitely more hateful than vipers and are in a most miserable condition." If that was not enough to make the point, he wanted to ensure that children would eventually be given feedback regarding their miserable condition. He emphasized that they are "naturally very senseless and stupid," and asked the question, "Why should we conceal the truth from them?"

Comparing infants to vipers seemed as popular an analogy as our practice of likening them to bundles of joy and cherubs. If their innate badness were not being highlighted, the quality of their mental processes might be slandered. "Curly, dimpled lunatics" was another description of infants that hardly gave parents an optimistic view of what lay in store.

The notion of infantile evil and depravity was rooted in a view of human nature that arose from the Puritan movement of the late sixteenth century. Reacting to what they saw as the excesses of most organized religion, the Puritans maintained a rigid distinction between what was "Godly" and what was "worldly." One's time on earth was an endless struggle; no matter how devout and pure you were, Satan was always lurking in the shadows to entice you away from the straight and narrow. What's more, Satan had an unfair advantage in the battle for your soul. The concept of original sin was a central part of the Puritan belief system and the baby was seen as possessing a will that should be feared more than respected. From the moment of birth, parents had to be sure the child was headed in the right direction. Obedience and conformity were considered essential; any sign of their absence could not be dismissed as a normal misdemeanor of childhood – it was an indication that the will, with all its evil propensities, was beginning to become unleashed.

In addition to a strong belief in innate badness, a prevalent view from Puritan times was that children were mini-adults. Today we liberally give our youngsters license to act in ways that would not be acceptable in adulthood. A preschooler's outrageous tale is accepted as a sign of her imagination rather than labeled a lie, and the sight of a toddler lying on the supermarket floor in the throes of a tantrum may evoke no more than relief that, for once, it isn't our child putting on the gala performance. The expression "kids will be kids" allows us to simultaneously communicate our tolerance of what they do and our hope that they will eventually stop doing it. "It's just a stage," we say, in an effort to reassure ourselves that we can count on maturation to give us at least some help in producing a well-adjusted adult. No separate set of expectations and standards existed, however, when children were viewed as scaled-down versions of adults.

Economic factors also contributed to this perception of children. To-

A three-year-old
gainfully employed as
a bird-scarer.

day child labor may be seen as exploitation, but not that long ago many families simply could not afford to support their children. Sons and daughters were needed to work in the home or had to contribute the meager earnings they could obtain from outside employment. Even very young children were more likely to be employed than schooled. Today, a three-year-old who can remember to hang up her coat, take her dishes to the sink, and flush – all on the same day – is applauded. Two hundred years ago the same child could have been employed as a bird-scarer or goose-girl and her six-year-old brother might be putting in fourteen-hour shifts at the local mill or underground mine. Youngsters finding themselves in such positions did function very much as adults, and in many important respects their roles could not be distinguished from those of their parents.

The Rule of the Rod

In combination, the belief in innate evil and the view that children should be adult-like created a climate in which strict discipline and intolerance for any behavior that did not conform to parental ideals flourished. Horace Bushnell carried such thinking into the Victorian era. As a professor and theologian he commanded much respect, and his *Views of Christian Nurture* was an influential book in the area of family values and child-rearing. He likened early development to the dawn of Creation and the struggles encountered by Adam and Eve. Virtue had long been lost; the serpent was an ever-present threat and it had to be assumed that the child had the same weakness for forbidden fruit as his ancestors. He warned that without the watchful eye of parents, the child would "plunge himself into evil by his own experiment."

Selective reading of the Bible provided the justification for using physical discipline in liberal measure. "Withhold not correction from the child; for if thou beatest him with the rod, he shall not die." The next verse from Proverbs essentially repeated the message: "Thou shalt beat him with a rod, and shalt deliver his soul from hell." Out of context, this approach can seem excessive, if not sadistic. But the task of delivering the child's soul from hell was part of the parent's obligation to God. While the viper might lie dormant within, so too did the potential to repent and earn salvation. The concerned parent also felt a sense of urgency; infant mortality was high and it was normal for a family to lose some of its youngest members before they even came close to maturity. Given this reality, it would be dangerous to assume that you had many years to mold a child who would be worthy of a place in heaven; often this was not the case.

Lying was close to the top of the list of offenses to be met with severe discipline. Truth and godliness were closely linked and lying was seen as a sign of inherent evil. Writing in early Victorian times, Reverend Hyde reminded parents that children "go astray as soon as they are born, speaking lies." He explained that the creative and determined infant did not have to wait until learning his first words before embarking on a career of deceit and treachery. "Lying" did not only refer to what a child might say with words. Crying might be construed as pretending to be hungry or hurt, and the offending infant or toddler could be whipped.

Disobedience was also a crime that had to be stamped out. Honoring your father and mother is one of the commandments and to disobey a parent was, therefore, to disobey God. There are accounts of extreme and brutal physical punishment used to beat children into submission. One is of a mother who wanted her sixteen-month-old to repeat "dear Mamma." This was apparently the way she had been taught to address her mother. The child refused and Mamma was not impressed. But after four hours of whippings, interspersed with periods of being shut in a closet, she finally complied. It would be easy to respond to such an incident with indignation and I would be the first to label it as abusive. At the same time, I would not want to assume that the mother was motivated by any cruel or hostile feelings towards her daughter; her primary motivation may well have been one of concern for her child's moral and spiritual welfare.

John Abbott wrote for "mothers in the common walks of life." His book, *The Mother at Home,* was published in 1834 and obedience was the cornerstone of his approach to child-rearing. Compliance was not, however, sufficient; he expected children to be open in their gratitude for the opportunity to demonstrate their obedience. Nothing short of "prompt and cheerful acquiescence" was acceptable and it was never too soon to begin teaching your offspring to appreciate discipline. As proof, he cited the case of a French man who had apparently taught a large number of canaries to march in platoons across the room. Suitably impressed, the reader was confronted with Abbott's pointed question, "Now can it be admitted that a child, fifteen months or two years of age is inferior to a canary-bird?" I wonder how many parents were ashamed to say that they would have to answer affirmatively and rushed out to purchase a canary as a role model for their unregimented offspring.

The child who did not march in step was to be dealt with promptly and severely. The parent had no choice but to "inflict bodily pain so steadily and so invariably that disobedience and suffering shall be indissolubly connected in the mind of the child." There was no room for leniency, second chances, or a suspended sentence; every command was to be followed immediately.

To illustrate his point, Abbott told the sad tale of Mary; she was a little girl who should have known better. Although she had been warned about playing with the family Bible, there came the sorry day when she ignored her mother's admonition and touched the Good Book. Mother knew just what to do. Unimpressed by Mary's contrition and assurances that the offense would never be repeated, she "seriously and calmly punishes her. She inflicts real pain – pain that will be remembered." Abbott is most sympathetic to the mother; in spite of being forced to punish her child, she finds it in her heart to forgive Mary as far as she can. The problem is that God was also upset. Not only did the wretched girl fail to follow the commandment about honoring one's parents, she also messed with His book. Reminded that God is not pleased, Mary falls to her knees and seeks divine forgiveness. In view of the enormity of the crime, mother has her repeat the exercise at bedtime to ensure that there is no doubt about her repentance.

Abbott gave other anecdotes of the "this hurts me more than it hurts you" ilk. The father who had to beat his son repeatedly because he refused to recite the alphabet almost relented and put away the rod. Knowing in his heart that such weakness on his part would ruin his son for life, he persisted. At long last the plaintive sounds of "A,B,C . . ." were heard and the father knew the lad was saved. Anticipating that the less stalwart parent might consider the punishment too severe, Abbott wrote, "Cruel! It was mercy and love – self-denying kindness."

The notion of spoiling the child by retiring the rod was carried to its extremes. Physicians talked of parents weeping over the graves of children who had died because of their lack of automatic obedience. Thousands were supposed to have perished after refusing to take medicine that, while foul-tasting, could have saved their lives. Ignoring their mothers' pleas to follow doctor's orders, they remained tight-lipped and succumbed to their ailments. Those that made it into adulthood only delayed their fate. Early permissiveness led to depravity and crime, and Abbott reported that "many an unhappy criminal has from the gallows traced back his course of guilt to when he commenced with disobedience to a mother's commands." The neglectful parent would also have to face her own punishment. Her lot was a "broken heart and an old age of sorrow." Such a fate was pitiful, but parents had only themselves to blame: "When you look upon your dissolute sons and ungrateful daughters, you must remember the time when you might have checked their evil propensities."

From Viper to Cherub

The early Victorian era was one of extremes. While support could be found for Puritan thinking, an entirely different view of childhood was also gaining ground. Jean-Jacques Rousseau was an eighteenth-century philosopher who revolutionized society's thinking about child-rearing. His book *Emile* was a parable illustrating his belief that children were born in a state of purity rather than wickedness. Its first line, "The Author of Nature makes all things good; man meddles with them and they become evil," was a declaration that shocked the establishment. The role of the parent was not to break the child's spirit and cast out evil, but to nurture his inborn benevolence.

Rousseau's ideas encouraged childcare writers to take a more relaxed approach to the topic of discipline. Angelic smiles were no longer a mask behind which a viper or dimpled lunatic lurked; they were the sign that you had indeed been blessed with one of God's cherubs. The "tiny God of the cradle" was one term used to describe the new arrival, and the *Ladies' Magazine* in 1833 referred to infants as innocent creatures who were "untouched by sin and untainted by the breath of corruption." Because of their almost divine state, young children were to be revered; it was even argued that there was an instinct in each parent's soul that impels us to lay all our treasures at our baby's feet.

If not aligned with the divine, the Victorians, with their love of flowery and excessive language, might refer to the infant in regal terms. The popular *Glaxo Baby Book* referred to the infant as "His Majesty the Child." Or you could be told that your infant was a ticket to bliss. Speaking of the mother's lot in life, an anonymous writer claimed, "ten thousand raptures thrill her bosom before a tooth is formed."

Compromise positions also emerged. For some experts the child was neither devil nor saint, but was born in a neutral condition. The belief in the "blank slate" was to be a popular idea, particularly among psychologists. Metaphors abounded. The young child was clay to be gently molded by loving hands or a plant to be watered and otherwise tended.

Another change was the gradual acceptance of childhood as a stage or series of stages. The more children were distinguished from adults, the more they could be subject to their own set of rules and standards. A young girl might act in a way that met with her parents' disapproval, not because she was bad, but because she did not have the ability to comprehend the reasoning of the adult world. This allowed for more tolerance and patience; kids were beginning to be just kids and expectations could be modified accordingly.

Throughout the nineteenth century these new views of children led the experts to modify the advice they gave regarding parenting. The influence of Christianity remained strong in their writing, but God was portrayed more as a benevolent father than a stern and vengeful deity. Respect was allowed to replace fear and there was more room for children's misbehavior to be tolerated or corrected instead of being met with alarm or exorcism through beating.

By the time Queen Victoria had her first child, the liberal use of physical punishment was being discouraged by a number of writers. *The Evil Tendencies of Corporal Punishment* was written by Lyman Cobb in 1847 and provided a detailed consideration of all the disadvantages associated with this type of discipline. The custom of lengthy imprisonment in closets or other equally as dark and frightening places also met with its critics. Parents were to govern with the authority earned through the way in which they directed and taught their children. They should teach by example and only resort to physical punishment if absolutely necessary. Rods, or their equivalent, were probably on most families' household inventory, but they were supposed to gather dust. In fact, a sign of a good parent was that you rarely, if ever, had to resort to beatings.

Balancing Freedom and Control

The more the Puritan beliefs and approaches concerning parenting lost ground, the more complicated the task of raising a child must have seemed. The gentler views that had emerged brought with them the need to balance authority and license, and temper control with a gradual increase in freedom. A child's will was no longer something to be broken – it had to be harnessed and directed. You were told to accept that children would not and could not be like adults, but how different could they be? If your toddler failed to preface every request with "dear Mamma," you knew there was still a chance she could turn out to be a well-adjusted adult and even earn a spot in paradise, but how broadly should you set the bounds of your tolerance? Complete obedience had been a simple concept; however difficult it might be to put into practice, at least there was no uncertainty as to the goal.

The dilemma facing parents was how to simultaneously provide the freedom children needed to develop and the discipline they required to do so in safe, socially acceptable ways. Just as repressive approaches to child-rearing were presented as damaging and unnecessary, so too was lack of sufficient parental guidance. The search for the middle ground was on.

This dilemma was illustrated throughout the Victorian era by the diverse impressions that can be obtained from the childcare literature. At times the advice was anything but permissive and was reminiscent of the harshness and rigidity that characterized Puritan times. In 1890 Doctor Francis Rankin published his manual *Hygiene of Childhood*. He was an unwavering member of the "old school" and he liked to get things off to an early start. He advised parents to get serious about discipline as soon as possible and stated with authority that "lessons in obedience can be and should be commenced during the early months of infancy, for children, like animals, will intuitively recognize the necessity of obedience." I am left with the inescapable conclusion that none of our five children was born with any intuition. For the Victorian parent who was more fortunate, however, the process of instilling discipline and self-control could begin almost immediately. Should you fail, your offspring was bound to become a "monster of selfishness, and a source of continual discomfort to himself and to those about him."

The great importance that was attached to infancy as the foundation for later life was a recurring theme in the literature. In its more extreme form, this belief led to very rigid approaches to childcare. Feeding schedules, for example, were seen as an issue of power and control rather than one of nutrition. The baby needed to follow a routine. If he did not, the parent was giving him his first lesson in disobedience. He would find that his protests and demands met with success. He could control his parents; they could not control him. There is, to my knowledge, no study linking demand feeding with delinquency, but the implication from some Victorian experts was that such a connection had to exist.

Babies have a somewhat narrow range of activities, but the experts asserted that self-control could be taught in other ways than just implementing a feeding schedule. For example, what should you do if your baby cried? Assuming hunger was not the issue, the question became one of deciding how much you should soothe, rock, or otherwise comfort your child. Some experts argued vehemently that the crying baby had to be ignored. Not to do so would be another example of how cherubs and angels could be transformed into monsters of selfishness. To buttress the argument, you might be told that crying should not be met with attempts to comfort the child as it was the infant's version of an aerobic work-out; weeping and wailing were beneficial as they exercised both the respiratory and circulatory systems.

Rocking chairs also met with disapproval from the highest authorities. Doctor Pye Henry Chavasse published his *Advice To a Wife and Counsel To a Mother* around 1879. The book was endorsed by no less than Queen Victoria's chief physician, Sir Charles Locock, and was popular among parents on both sides of the Atlantic in the latter part of the era. He argued that rocking encouraged infants to be dependent on the mother rather than learning how to soothe or settle themselves; the child's sleep would also be feverish and disturbed. As far as he was concerned, the chairs were used by lazy and incompetent mothers and "the sooner they are banished from the nursery the better will it be for the infant community." Even worse was the combination of rocking and singing lullabies; this could only be described as a "miserable and depressing performance." I take exception to this. My middle of the night rendition of *Rock-a-Bye Baby* may have needed work, but it was not that bad.

Bowel and bladder control was another example of a stage of development that was often construed as a matter of discipline. For the Victorian parent, attempts at toilet training might begin within the first month or so of life. You were told that placing an infant on a pot at regular intervals – usually following feeding – would instill good habits. I have not found any accounts of how successful the parents were who followed advice of this nature, but I suspect many experienced a great deal of frustration and began to doubt their ability to teach their children self-control.

Doctor Emmett Holt was a pediatrician who lamented the drift away from the Puritanical approaches to what he saw as an epidemic of sentimental mush. He was best known for his book, *Care and Feeding of Children*, which was first published towards the end of the Victorian era. After reading Holt you are left with the impression of the nursery as a boot camp with the parent as the sergeant-major who has the warmth and humor of a crustacean. Not only was crying to be ignored, but also any mother caught rocking her infant or playing with a baby under the age of six months was up for a court martial. Sentimentality was out; regularity was the order of the day and the objective was to have the child fully regimented within the first few months of life. He also had a particular aversion to kissing. Parents should refrain from the practice as much as possible. The underlying belief seemed to be that children would construe physical affection as a sign of weakness and would fail to develop respect for authority.

I am not suggesting that the topics discussed by the childcare writers were trivial. Sooner or later most of us will expect our offspring to conform to the routine of set meal times. Any parent who wants the luxury of free time to do the housework, or aspires to something close to a good night's sleep, also learns that crying babies occasionally have to be left to sort things out for themselves. Toilet training is similarly an issue that parents need to consider. After twenty-eight years as a parent my major ambition has become that of reaching the stage in my life where I no longer have to assume responsibility for, or display interest in, any other person's bowel or bladder activities. What characterized the more conservative Victorian childcare literature, however, was its message of urgency and the inflexibility of its demands. The brutality that had occurred when the rod was the enforcer had gone, but the advice given created a new type of authoritarian, if not oppressive parenting.

But this was only one side of the debate or dilemma. Not all advice-givers shared the belief in early regimentation in order to imprint self-control on the minds of infants. The notion of feeding babies on demand had its proponents and the idea of trying to put infants on a pot before they could even hold their heads up was by no means universally accepted. In contrast to the "crying promotes moral and physical development" school of thought, the "cuddle and coo" movement also found its supporters. The mother confronted with a crying daughter did not have to worry that picking her up almost guaranteed she would refuse to serve tea to the vicar or practise her deportment exercises as a young lady. Having been told that infants were naturally inclined to cheerfulness, you were advised that, if they cried, something had to be wrong and you should, therefore, try your best to soothe them. As was so often the case, this advice, although permissive for its time, came with a stern warning. If you did not intervene in this way, a crying baby would become terminally miserable and you would be the cause of her bad temper.

Throughout the nineteenth century examples of this greater tolerance and permissiveness can be found. A prominent writer chose a title for his book that would reflect his strong aversion to the more authoritarian approaches. Jacob Abbott's *Gentler Measures in the Management of the Young* was published in 1871. Reviewing family life of his day, he concluded that "children are not generally indulged enough" and recommended that they should be given the "greatest freedom of action." He was highly critical of the use of corporal punishment, particularly when this involved violence such as whippings. He argued that punishment of this nature was potentially dangerous to the child as it could damage the "extremely delicate and almost embryonic condition of the cerebral and nervous organization."

Chavasse also pulled no punches in his condemnation of physical discipline and other methods of control that engendered fear. The custom of whipping that John Abbott had called "self-denying kindness" was now "cruel, cowardly, and brutal." Those supporting corporal punishment in the schools received a similar tongue-lashing; this practice was "revolting, disgusting, and demoralizing." As far as he was concerned, beating children destroyed rather than built character; it created insecurity, resentment, and fearfulness in the child, not respect.

Kate Douglas Wiggin used the type of image that characterized her most famous children's book, *Rebecca of Sunnybrook Farm*, when casting her vote for the gentler approach. A great advocate for nurturing children's playfulness and creativity in an atmosphere of tolerance, she asserted that "a child has a right to a genuine, free, serene, healthy, bread-and-butter childhood."

The child who was given freedom of action could not be expected to be a perfect little gentleman or lady. Reverend Charles Frederic Goss had a particularly soft spot for boys. *Husband, Wife, and Home* was published at the end of the era and was read widely in North America and England. He compared boys to spirited colts who needed to find their gait. Parents were the jockeys; they were there to guide and coax, but had to be careful not to break the boys' spirit. Allowing boys room to maneuver made it inevitable that they would periodically fall from grace as they experimented with living: "The poor little chaps are playing with violent explosives, and it isn't strange that they get blown up now and then." The pinnacle of rationalization was reached with his statement that "in most little rascals, badness is only misdirected goodness." Now that's tolerance!

Confronted with the likelihood that your offspring would make a hobby of misdirecting his goodness, you were encouraged to develop a sense of humor. "Playfulness" would become "naughtiness" at times, and although parents might correct the offending behavior, inwardly they could smile at their children's antics. The snake-in-the-grass of the Puritan age was now a mischievous monkey that would keep you not only hopping, but also entertained.

Goss wrote extensively about this more gentle and relaxed approach to child-rearing. He was among those experts who encouraged parents to cultivate their nurturing instincts and express love and affection openly with their children. "Home life ought to be full of kisses and caresses. Kisses are like grains of gold and silver found upon the ground: of no value in themselves, but precious as showing that a mine is near." Embraces and kisses were the panacea for a thousand ills and were the "heavenly manna needed by children and parents alike." Despite his calling, he added, "I had almost as soon see children brought up without the ten commandments as without embraces and kisses."

Home life was also to be full of kind deeds, "for they are the deepest and most reliable manifestations of love." How people referred to family members would be another way to convey their feelings. Nicknames were recommended. The ones my brother and I had for each other would have been unacceptable; in two words or less we could imply that the other was completely devoid of all known endearing qualities. The pet name of choice for the Victorian household, on the other hand, was "sweetheart," and Goss's advice was to "butter your tongues. Let your words drop honey." Just as affection was depicted as an essential part of family life, its absence was portrayed as a critical component of children's ills. The parent as disciplinarian was by no means outlawed, but if the discipline were cold and stern it would create an emotional vacuum that would deprive children of the closeness and intimacy they needed.

The gentler approaches to child-rearing were, however, entirely optional. The prevailing view was that the parents, and especially the father, had the right to run their domestic affairs without interference from outside persons or institutions. Professor Francis Wayland wrote on this matter in *The Elements of Moral Science* (1874). He noted that the Old Testament decreed that children were to submit to their parents' will ("Honor thy father and thy mother") and that this directive had been repeated in the New ("Children, obey your parents in the Lord, for this is right.") These verses became the basis for his "Law of Children." They had four obligations to their mother and father: obedience, reverence, affection, and support in their old age. Wayland was nonetheless critical of insensitive and harsh parents, but was forced to concede that the mistreated child had no choice but to accept what fate had ordained. To question or rebel would only be adding another grave sin to the one perpetrated by the parent and expose the transgressor to "special and peculiar judgements" including the curse of God. By comparison, suffering in silence was the option of choice and the only consolation for the child was knowing that submission to authority was "the most honorable and delightful exhibition of character that can be exhibited by the young."

A Beautiful Blending

There were writers who attempted to combine aspects of the law-and-order and more permissive schools of thinking. Goss, for example, took great pains to create a unified approach to child-rearing that included the best of the old and new. He talked about the "beautiful blending of sternness with gentleness." Such a blending was not necessarily easy to perfect and he provided a sympathetic and insightful discussion of how difficult it is to be "as hard as steel and immovable as granite when a child needs to be curbed and chastened, and to be as fluid as water and as caressing as air in all those moments when it needs sympathy and tenderness." Such a goal had to be pursued, however: "if you are not the first, the child will trample you under its feet, and if you are not the second, it will consider you an iceberg."

As tempting as it might have been, parents were warned not to return to a simpler and more authoritarian style of child-management when faced with the problems of this approach. Goss recognized that discipline could be relatively easy in the earliest years and argued that very young children had a natural tendency to assume that their parents were infallible and would look upon them as "the incarnation of perfection." The reason I have yet to notice this tendency in any of my children is probably attributable to the fact that it is a very short-lived phase. According to Goss, children quickly become aware of any deficiencies and faults their parents might possess and, from this point on, authority is only be retained if it is deserved.

Although Jacob Abbott tends to be associated with the more permissive approaches to parenting, his book contains many illustrations of how parents were to combine "gentler measures" with unwavering discipline. He left no doubt in his readers' minds that parents were in charge. Compliance was to be secured by "submission to authority – that absolute and almost unlimited authority which all parents are commissioned by God and nature to exercise over their offspring." The trick was to establish and maintain this authority without being harsh. In many respects the image of the ideal parent created in his book corresponds to the one often portrayed in more recent literature. Above all, Abbott's parent is loving and caring. She is patient and understanding, and while she will not hesitate to express her disapproval of her offspring's behavior or attitudes when so warranted, she does so in a way that also communicates respect.

Abbott's book is filled with illustrations and detailed descriptions of how the gentler measures could be applied. Louisa, for example, had lied about the number of apples she had consumed in order to obtain another. Instead of a beating or a period of solitary confinement in the closet, her mother took her aside for a talk. So verbally proficient and creative was her mother that she had no difficulty launching into a lengthy parable concerning the perils of falsehoods. Whereas my lectures have evoked only heavy sighs and eye-rolling from my children, Louisa was nothing but suitably impressed: she "paused a moment, looked in her mother's face, and then, reaching up to put her arms around her mother's neck, she said, 'Mamma, I am determined never to tell you another wrong story as long as I live.'"

Abbott emphasized early training, but not for the purpose of breaking the child's will. Rather, if the parent were consistent from day one in establishing rules together with mild punishments for transgressions, there would never be a need to resort to harsh and excessive forms of control. He acknowledged that some parents were not as skilled as others and begrudgingly conceded that physical discipline might have to be used as a last resort: "Better that a child be trained and governed by the rod than not trained and governed at all." He made it clear, however, that the rod was more a symbol of the parent's failure than a sign of the child's badness. Dedicated and consistent application of the gentler measures would "make the years of their childhood, years of tranquillity and happiness, both to ourselves and to them."

I am sure I am not alone in having had a picture of the cold, rigid, and distant Victorian parent who never cracked a smile, was convinced that

children should be seen and not heard, and lived by the motto "spare the
rod and spoil the child." It would be a mistake, however, to consider this
stereotype characteristic of the Victorian approach to discipline. The period was one in which ideas regarding child-management became far
more complex than had been the case in earlier times. The experts talked
of control and obedience, but they also argued that affection, patience,
and tolerance were ingredients essential to children's development. The
list of qualities needed by parents seemed to expand and writers such as
Goss, Chavasse, and Abbott began creating a new image of the ideal parent that continues to be found in modern childcare literature. Parents
needed to be strong, fair, and loving. They should show a "sweet reasonableness" and teach their children through their own good behavior as actions "speak more volubly, forcefully, and effectually than words can,
however eloquent they be." They should be allowed to make noise and
make messes, and a mischievous child was to be preferred to an idle one.
Patience and affection were to replace the harshness and rigidity of the authoritarian parent, and love was to be "the guide and rule of all you do and
say." Such advice hardly seems out of place today.

3. Play and Leisure

NOBODY TODAY would question that play is very much part of childhood. This is, however, a view that was not necessarily accepted in earlier times. The Puritans had developed a strict code of rules and mores that was directed towards most forms of worldly pleasures. The emphasis on observance of the Sabbath, for example, had far-reaching implications for the working person who would typically be employed for long hours from Monday to Saturday. Sunday was often the only opportunity for relaxation, but the chance of actually enjoying oneself would have been minimal. Although taking a quiet stroll in a park might not be seen by most people as succumbing to one's wild and primitive impulses, it was on the list of banned activities. You could read the Good Book, but little else as, according to the *Evangelical Magazine* of 1793, "all novels, generally speaking, are instruments of abomination and ruin." Theater-going was, of course, not even to be considered and was ranked equally with drunkenness with respect to its level of sin. As for ballet, the moral dangers were unthinkable. A prominent politician even suggested that a French plot to overthrow Britain included infiltrating the

country with ballet dancers. The thought of undercover agents clad in tu-
tus intrigues me.

Puritan thinking remained influential at the beginning of the Victorian era and there were parents who believed that forms of play were
either pointless or contrary to the goals of godliness and single-minded
devotion to hard work and pure thoughts. As childhood began to be seen
as a distinct phase of development, and with the mellowing of attitudes towards child-rearing, opinions shifted and play gradually acquired acceptance as a natural and desirable pursuit. Economic factors also played a
role; as families became smaller, more time and money could be devoted
to recreation.

While play became more a part of children's lives, it was not treated as
an area that should be left solely in the hands of the parents. The purpose
and impact of play became a topic that weighed heavily on the minds of
the experts. For some, play was no more than a natural and joyful impulse
that should be encouraged. As Goss explained, "to run and roll, to tumble
and dance, are as natural to children as breathing and eating. Their antics
have no more purpose than those of a goat. And therein lies their divine
loveliness." Mischief might also be condoned and was described as an instinct to be restrained and perhaps chastened, although never beaten out
of the child. But, as will be discussed throughout this chapter, there were
definite limitations on how children's playful and mischievous impulses
should be expressed. Play was, in fact, a moral and physical minefield and
parents had to be educated regarding its perils.

Nursery Rhymes and All That Nonsense

Our daughter has just learned the hard truth about the Tooth Fairy. At
seven years of age, Kiera was beginning to wonder why any creature,
however magical, would check under the pillows of all the children in the
world each night in order to add to her collection of discarded teeth.
Kiera's questions became more difficult to answer. For example, where
does the Tooth Fairy live and what does she really do with her immense
collection? The Tooth Fairy was beginning to be a thorn in our side. For
each of Kiera's questions we had to invent an answer and make sure we remembered what we had said just in case the issue was raised again. Root-

ing around under the pillow in the dark trying to find a minuscule molar without waking her was also an unwelcome challenge and not exactly a relaxing way to end a long day.

Then one morning I was forced to reveal all. We had once again forgotten to leave the money under her pillow and I was in the process of pretending it had fallen under her bed. (For the uninitiated, this emergency procedure involves concealing the money in your hand, crawling around on the floor, and announcing a successful find while accusing your child of being a restless sleeper who must have knocked the loot out of the bed.) But Kiera was ready for me. "I've already checked the floor," she said, stopping me dead in my tracks. As I tried to muster all my powers of creativity to find a solution to a very tricky problem, she looked me squarely in the eye and asked, "Is there really a Tooth Fairy?" I stalled for time, trying to recall how the reporter in that famous short story had managed to con Virginia into a life-long belief in Santa Claus, but nothing came to mind. When all else fails in such situations, you have nothing left but the truth. So I broke the news to her, feeling somewhat awkward and sheepish as I tried to assure her that she really did have honest and trustworthy parents in spite of the fact that we had told her lie upon lie to reinforce a preposterous myth. To my surprise she did not seem the least bit concerned. Having secured a guarantee that she was still entitled to financial compensation for each lost tooth, she hurried off to breakfast and has not raised the topic since.

We often lie to children. The word "lie" may seem a bit strong, but it is a common practice to deliberately deceive our offspring. The standard Santa, Tooth Fairy, and Easter Bunny are the prime examples. We also teach them rhymes about dishes eloping with spoons and pies baked with singing blackbirds. If confronted with questions regarding whether or not cows can actually jump over the moon we will probably answer truthfully, but we often see the belief in the magical and whimsical as a harmless, if not enviable part of young people's imagination.

This view was not, however, typical of earlier periods in history. The Puritans had warned of the dangers of any departure from the truth and examples of similar concerns can be found throughout Victorian times and into the twentieth century. In addition to the impact on the child's spiritual well-being, fantasy could have dire psychological and physical consequences. Doctor Marie Stopes practiced medicine at the turn of the century and is most remembered for her pioneering work as an advocate for family planning, birth control, and sex education. She also ventured into other areas of domestic life and had strong opinions regarding the harmful effects of early fables, such as telling children they had been delivered to the home in a doctor's bag or had been flown in by a stork. These and equally as fanciful notions, such as abandonment under gooseberry bushes, were nothing short of "pernicious lies." Although the young child might not remember one word of what was said, "the effects on his outlook will be deep." It was argued that, even though there were no initial signs of harm, the lie would remain in the unconscious and cause inestimable damage in later life. "In this way infinite injury has been done to the whole human stock."

Rankin had particular concerns about nursery rhymes, although he believed the risk to the child was physical and mental rather than moral. He argued that "by committing to memory too many nursery rhymes the mind is overtaxed and harmful results are sure to follow." He was quite specific about the mechanism involved: the strain on the child would deplete the body's "nerve-force" and have long-term and irreversible effects on both mental and physical development. He reminded the reader of the increasing incidence of insanity in the population and, by the end of the chapter, parents who owned a copy of *Mother Goose* must have been overwhelmed by feelings of guilt at having condemned their offspring to being physically stunted and mentally deranged.

Fairy Tales and Mind-Improving Literature

At times the attitudes towards fairy tales and similar stories met with disapproval that was equally as intense as that directed towards childhood myths and nursery rhymes. *Aesop's Fables* evoked outright disgust from some quarters because of the way in which human qualities and abilities were attributed to lowly beasts. "As spiritual people we look down with such contempt upon the man who would in anything compare us with the lower animals," wrote Harriett Martineau in *Harpers Monthly* in 1850. Her article was titled "How to Make Home Unhealthy" and she wanted it known that, fiction though they may be, stories that failed to maintain the distinction between humans and the rest of the animal kingdom would harm more than they would instruct or entertain.

Although parents were warned of the dangers of exposing young minds to such grave distortions and departures from reality, fairy tales never appeared to lose their popularity. The most renowned had been written long before Victorian times; many editions of Charles Perrault's classics, such as *Cinderella* and *Sleeping Beauty,* appeared throughout the nineteenth century, as did the works of the Brothers Grimm. Unlike today, however, fairy tales were often read to children to provide moral training rather than to entertain. Perrault, for example, concluded each tale with a moral. The moral of *Red Riding Hood* was that "children, especially pretty, nicely brought-up young ladies, ought never to talk to strangers." As for Sleeping Beauty, she reinforced the notion that "a brave, rich, handsome husband is a prize well worth waiting for." Perrault conceded, however, that "no modern woman would think it was worth waiting for a hundred years" for such a prize.

One of our modern-day concerns regarding the media is the potential risk of exposing children to material that, while drawing their attention, may be upsetting and frightening for them. Reading the original, pre-Disney versions of fairy tales, however, is a reminder that children were exposed to the macabre and brutal long before *Nightmare on Elm Street. Hop O' My Thumb* (later to be known as *Tom Thumb*) is a prime example. Tom was the youngest son of a poor woodcutter and his wife. Times were hard and the cupboard was bare. Rather than watch the children starve in front of their eyes, they decided it would be easier for all concerned if the boys were abandoned in the forest. Tom – although berated by his parents because of his assumed stupidity – was wise to their tricks and managed to thwart the first attempt at *post-hoc* family planning. Not to be deterred, the woodcutter and his wife set out once more and took them to the "densest and deepest part of the forest. Once they had arrived, they slipped away through the undergrowth." Things weren't looking too good for Tom and his brothers, and they were soon to get much worse. In the days before Block Parents, you took your chances when you knocked on a stranger's door. As luck would have it, they stumbled onto a cottage that was home to the local ogre. His wife warned them that her spouse was "a horrid ogre, who eats babies," but Tom, who seemed determined to prove his parents' view of how smart he was, decided they should accept her invitation to stay for the night. Fortunately for Tom and his brothers, the ogre *was* stupid, as well as being short-sighted. He arose in the middle of the night to butcher the boys so they would be ready for the table the next day. In error, he slit the throats of his seven sleeping daughters, who were discovered in the morning, dead and "swimming in blood." Tom, who finally realizes that his choice of accommodation was less than desirable, engineers their escape. Having been treated to a bedtime story that guaranteed nightmares for weeks to come, the child was presented with the moral – namely, that even a "puny weakling who is despised, jeered at and mocked" can make good in the end.

Cautionary verse also employed blood and gore to point out the perils of misbehavior. Accounts were told in rhyme of a boy who ran away from his nurse only to be eaten by a lion and a little girl who burned to

Victorian bedtime reading: A short-sighted ogre mistakenly slits the throats of his sleeping daughters.

death as a result of telling dreadful lies. Doctor Heinrich Hoffmann's poems were also a hit in English as well as their original German version. Apparently Doctor Hoffmann was out Christmas shopping for his young son in 1844 and was dismayed by the lack of suitable literature. His only solution was to write a book himself. *Struwwelpeter* was billed as a collection of "merry stories and funny pictures." The definition of merry was obviously different in those days. After introducing the reader to a budding young psychopath, Frederick, whose pastimes included tearing the wings off flies and killing birds, we hear of yet another girl being burnt to ashes – this time because of playing with matches. Augustus was less of a miscreant, but he too met an early death because of failing to eat his soup. The goriest of them all is *The Story of Little Suck-a-Thumb*. Conrad had it coming to him. His mother had warned him time and time again that little boys who sucked their thumbs were in line for a visit from the "great tall tailor" and his "great sharp scissors." But would Conrad listen? His end was inevitable:

> The door flew open, in he ran,
> The great, long, red-legged scissor man,
> Oh! children, see! the tailor's come
> And caught out little Suck-a-Thumb.
> Snip! Snap! Snip! the scissors go;
> And Conrad cries out "Oh! Oh! Oh!"
> Snip! Snap! Snip! They go so fast,
> That both his thumbs are off at last.

Conrad's thumb-sucking problem is finally cured.

Among the ranks of Hoffmann's characters, I suppose Conrad was one of the more fortunate. But while he did survive to tell the tale of his ordeal, mamma's response was little more than, "I told you so."

The Victorian parent did have access to other books that were of the mind-improving variety without such R-rated contents. In the first part of the century, poems and stories that contained a simple, direct, and reality-based moral message were popular. Little children were depicted as struggling in a world full of pitfalls and traps. To prevail they clung to the basic principles of virtue, truth, and obedience to their parents. If they strayed, they suffered, but if they were strong the book guaranteed them a happy ending. For the more tragic hero or heroine, their just rewards might be deferred to the afterlife, but better to have endured hardship for a spot in paradise than meet the fate of those who gave in to temptation.

Jacob Abbott wrote children's books as well as authoring his popular childcare manual. His best-known contribution was the Rollo series. Rollo exemplified the virtuous boy who aspired to all the qualities of the ideal Victorian male. He was industrious and pious, and had a deep respect for authority. He was also very, very boring. In making such a condemnation I admit I am revealing my bias for children's stories that can at least kindle a flame in one's imagination and occasionally leave the reader enthralled and excited. After a few pages of a Rollo book I become obsessed with the fantasy that he would suddenly do or say something totally outrageous, but he never fails to stick to the straight and narrow.

Abbott's less-remembered anti-hero, Rodolphus, was a much livelier character. The poor lad never had a hope of making it. His parents meant well, but they were pushovers. When "Rolf" wanted pet rabbits, he got them in spite of his mother's opposition; when he wanted to stay up late he would make such a fuss that his parents would indulge him. This was certainly no way to raise a child and Abbott spells out the moral of the story at the beginning of chapter one: "The manner in which indulgence and caprice on the part of the parent lead to the demoralization and ruin of the child is illustrated by the history of Rodolphus."

It quickly becomes obvious that Rodolphus will have to pay dearly for not following Rollo's example. Bad training has damaged his character and he simply has no moral fiber. Sadly, he becomes "a source of continual trial and trouble to his mother, though she did not know one half of his evil deeds." Given to many bad habits, he proved to be beyond redemption. A cast of characters takes turns trying to set him straight, but to no avail. No sooner has he promised to reform than he is sneaking out of the house under cover of darkness to join the gang for a "night of carousals and wickedness under a barn." The reader is never told exactly what goes on when people carouse under barns, but Rodolphus clearly had a good time. He eventually realizes that he is a scoundrel, but by then it's too late. Before he runs away to hide his shame and rid his family of his presence, he leaves a note in which he acknowledges that he has condemned himself to a life of depravity. Not content to leave us with this picture of the doomed Rodolphus, Abbott points out that the note was poorly written and contained many spelling errors – a reflection, no doubt, of his including truancy in his list of crimes.

Abbott also produced a series for girls that matched the dreariness of the Rollo collection. The Lucy books presented "an account of the gradual progress made by our little heroine in the acquisition of knowledge and in the formation of character." And very gradual it was. Much of the first six pages of *Lucy On The Sea-Shore,* for example, is devoted to a description of Lucy's bookcase and her agonizing over which books to place on a particular shelf. A later chapter, "The Rescue," sounds promising. Perhaps Lucy was to be saved from drowning or rescued from a ledge on a dangerously high cliff. No such luck. She and her friends were trying to find their way home and came across a herd of cows who did not want to move aside. A gentleman appeared who walked through the midst of the docile beasts and escorted the girls to their destination. It may well be the case that reshelving books and circumnavigating herds of cows were about as exciting as life ever became for the middle- or upper-class girls of the time, but the thought of providing some escape or entertainment did not seem to enter the author's mind. Abbott's goal was clear and singular. His books were written "with a view to their moral influence on the hearts and dispositions of the readers. They present quiet and peaceful pictures of happy domestic life, portraying generally such conduct, and expressing such sentiments and feelings as it is desirable to exhibit and express in the presence of children."

Maria Edgeworth was an eighteenth-century author who was revered by Abbott. Her books were common in nursery libraries in the Victorian era and I am sure Lucy displayed them prominently on her shelves. One edition of her collected works ran to eighteen volumes and her *Moral Tales* were particularly well known. Through a combination of "innocent amusement and early instruction" she set out to prepare the young for the duties and responsibilities of life. She was careful not to arouse any passions in the child and, although an advocate of reading, was concerned that play could readily become too exciting. Her intent was not to "inflame the imagination" and there seems little doubt that she accomplished this goal.

As the Victorian era progressed, the characters in children's literature underwent a significant change. The earlier books had reflected the view that children were to be as adult-like as possible; their mission was to imitate the attitudes and behaviors of their elders and betters. With the increasing acceptance of childhood as a qualitatively different phase of development, there was more room for the young heroine or hero to have a distinct personality. Some historians have also argued that, with the growth of industry and commerce, there was a need to encourage the development of independent thinking and risk-taking. Characters emerged in children's stories who took the world on rather than follow a script written by the old guard. Luke Larkin was such a character. The hero of Horatio Alger's novels, he had an enthusiastic following during the last four decades of the nineteenth century. Luke triumphed because he was brave, smart, and self-reliant. His efforts allowed him to rise above his humble origins and he conquered adversity through his endless resourcefulness. The conclusion of Luke's adventures in *Struggling Upward* (1890) was characteristic of this type of inspirational literature. Luke had faced numerous hardships and had prevailed against a succession of thieves and villains. Alger reminds us that Luke "struggled upward from a boyhood of privation and self-denial into a youth and manhood of prosperity and honor. There has been some luck about it, I admit, but after all he is indebted for most of his good fortune to his own good qualities."

Parents' choice of books also reflected the gender stereotyping that remained prevalent. Like their male counterparts, heroines became more adventuresome, but they did not relinquish their goal of becoming good wives and mothers. Novels reinforced the restrictions placed on women's roles and activities. At the same time, the experts cautioned against too much emphasis on romance; the story line should ensure that the girl eventually reached the altar, but she had to maintain her virtue en route. Any literature that crossed the line from modesty into passion would be dangerous to the health. Romance novels were considered to be a major cause of uterine disease because of their damaging effects on women's already delicate physiology. Today such an idea might seem absurd; it would be akin to gynecologists routinely asking patients if they had ever indulged in Harlequin romances. We live in an era where books describing women's sexual fantasies have become best-sellers. The Victorian parent, on the other hand, was advised that stories containing anything more exciting than a flowery, hands-off declaration of affection would be dangerous, if not life-threatening. It was critical, therefore, to prevent girls from developing the "novel-reading habit," as it was labeled by Ingrad Harting. Writing for a magazine in the latter part of the century, Mrs. Harting paints a pitiful picture of the girl whose addiction to novels leads her into a world of silly dreams and fantasies. Far from improving the mind, it becomes enfeebled: "Her mind becomes absolutely incapable of any mental process involving the slightest exertion."

Not even a cursory discussion of nineteenth-century children's literature should omit reference to the arrival of the periodicals that survived

Moths, Mohicans, & Malay pirates: samples from the Boy's Own Paper that no reader could resist.

for many generations. *The Boy's Own Paper* first appeared in the 1870s and was quickly followed by its companion, *The Girl's Own Paper*. The preview for the 1897–98 *B.O.P.* promised to enthrall the subscriber: "Not a dull line in it," was the unabashed promise, along with the prediction that "no boy will be able to resist its attractions." Definitions of "dull" and "resistible" must have been very different in those days. Following this introductory hype was a list of upcoming plates and stories, including, "Our British Moths and British Beetles" and "Irish Regiments of the British Army." I suspect that many a boy flipped past these gems to the much more intriguing "A White Slave's Adventures in the Alligator Land."

In keeping with the gender stereotyping prevalent in other literature,

The Girl's Own Paper: *afternoon teacakes and other topics of "intense interest to young ladies."*

the *G.O.P.* was in the business of creating the next generation of home-
makers. Its contents also reflected the fact that many girls were far more
involved in domestic activities than is often the case today. The regular
features included recipes for family meals and household hints. Having
learned that the creative cook can work wonders with mutton and stale
bread, the reader was told how to make her own laundry gloves, prepare a
cordial to treat dysentery, and contribute to the family income by following the series, "Profitable Duck-Keeping." Notwithstanding its support
for the traditional role of girls and women, *G.O.P.* was willing to move
with the times. The "Competition For Professional Girls" invited essays
on personal career choices and accomplishments. Prizewinners included a
nurse, folk-lore collector, organist, and publisher's clerk. The post-
mistress was particularly excited about her vocation and, although commenting on her twelve-hour work day, expressed nothing but gratitude at
having Sunday off each week.

The Great Outdoors

I live in a part of the world where for at least half of the year outdoor activities are an invitation to hypothermia and frostbite. Yet we persist in
bundling up our youngsters so they can skate, toboggan, and otherwise
have fun in the fresh air. There seems to be an engrained belief in the value
of outdoor activities. We justify it as a sign of parental concern regarding
our children's health and welfare. I wonder, however, if our motivation is
somewhat less altruistic than we care to admit. As the person in our family who nobly offers to stay behind and get the hot chocolate ready for
their return, I suspect the fact that I have the house to myself for an hour
or two has some relevance.

Most Victorians shared this enthusiasm for the great outdoors. Fresh
air was seen as a vital aspect of maintaining health, as well as offering a
mental diversion. When advising frequent outdoor activity, Goss commented on the value of having a lake within reach for skating, swimming,
and fishing. So enthused was he about this topic that he added, "If I could
make a world, I should plant a little lake by the side of every cradle." But
outdoor activities had to be chosen with due consideration to certain laws
of health. Kite-flying was uplifting – it symbolized the raising of the spir-

its and cast the child's eyes heavenward. It also maintained an upright posture, which was seen as promoting health. A game of marbles (either outdoors or inside), on the other hand, was an entirely different matter. Crouching down like an animal evoked the lower instincts and was as unhealthy as it was unseemly.

Chavasse also wanted children outside as much as possible. In keeping with modern soap commercials, he encouraged mothers to look with affection and tolerance at their offspring as they returned from play in their soiled and stained clothing. He went so far as to sanction the making of dirt pies and rolling around with children on the ground. He had little time for the sedentary, studious child: "Do not on any account allow him to sit any length of time at a table, amusing himself with books." A youngster so discovered was to be directed outdoors with due haste "to make the blood bound merrily through the vessels."

There were, however, experts who were loathe to recommend most forms of outdoor recreation because of the risk that it would be engaged in to excess. "Skating, rowing, racing, base-ball, foot-ball, dancing and most other exercises of the sort, are more often harmful than otherwise,"

Aerobic workout for young ladies: skipping with grace and dignity.

wrote Doctor John Kellogg in his 1886 manual, *Plain Facts for Old and Young*. He also advised against swinging on trapezes, but endorsed "riding in a lumber wagon over a corduroy road" as a safe form of exercise.

For girls, there was a gradual acceptance of their participation in outdoor activities beyond the ladylike stroll in the park. Chavasse endorsed skipping, but by far his most-favored sport for girls was croquet. He raved about its growing popularity and claimed that the sport had "improved both the health and the happiness of womankind more than any game ever before invented." The creator of the game was unknown, but Chavasse wanted him placed high on a pedestal: "The man who invented croquet has deserved greater glory than many philosophers."

Skating and hoop-rolling were more controversial as they were classed as boys' sports. Lydia Child wrote on this topic in the 1830s and was quite advanced for her times in her support of girls sharing such activities. But parents were left with the feeling that it was still not altogether proper. It was important to ensure that there was no public display of unfeminine behavior; hoop-rolling and the like had to be "pursued within the inclosure of a garden or court" when engaged in by the fairer sex. Above all, a careful balance had to be maintained between the need for physical exercise and the requirement that girls conform to the ideal of gentle femininity.

Doctor William Alcott, who wrote the *Gift Book for Young Ladies*, also favored keeping the girls behind the garden wall, and he reminded them of how suited they were to horticulture: "Your fondness of your garden is very favorable. Your flowers, your vines, your fruit-trees, will all of them minister to your amusement." To accommodate the more adventuresome girl who sought exertion beyond weeding, watering, and pruning, "an occasional ramble with a friend in pursuit of rare flowers, plants, minerals, insects, or birds" was acceptable. Recognizing that the well-bred young lady of his day might be shocked at such talk, he offered reassurance that his ideas had been approved by the ultimate authority: "Should you compromise your dignity and walk a little more rapidly or even run and clap your hands, do not think you have committed a sin unpardonable in Heaven's court."

The assumption that girls were endowed with a less robust constitution, although incorrect, was a way of reinforcing for parents the need to keep their daughters within the bounds of propriety. Boys, on the other hand, could exert themselves with abandon, and proving their strength and stamina allowed them to establish their masculinity. They could even sweat without shame; for girls this would have been vulgar, to say the least, and no more than a "glow" was recommended.

Girls at play: have fun while maintaining decorum.

The restrictions placed on girls did not have to deprive them of the opportunity to be fit. Kellogg pointed out that it was not necessary for them to leave the confines of the home to obtain all the exercise they needed. Extolling the virtues of domestic servitude, he asserted that "general housework is admirably adapted to bring into play all the different muscles of the body, while affording such a variety of different exercises and such frequent change that no part need be very greatly fatigued." Although Kellogg does not discuss any details of his personal life, a recommendation of this sort could only come from someone who has never washed floors or cleaned toilets.

The separation between the sexes decreased over time. Mixed skating parties became acceptable (suitably chaperoned, of course). Girls also joined boys on the courts after lawn tennis was introduced towards the end of the nineteenth century. But the Victorians were quick to see the perils of new trends. The sailboat is a case in point. If I had realized its potential to add excitement to my adolescence, I would have saved desperately to invest in one. Well into the twentieth century parents were cautioned against sailing as an activity for girls. The bracing winds and challenge of the open sea were all well and good, but a male was needed to captain the vessel. Imagine what might happen if the wind dropped and the vessel were becalmed. While the surrounding waters might be still, a tide of passion could swamp the occupants. A sailboat, you were told, was nothing short of a moral trap.

One of my favorite examples of how the experts thought they were duty-bound to pass judgment on recreational pursuits and activities involves bicycles. Towards the end of the century bicycle-riding became popular for girls and boys. In case you were unaware, a bicycle has profound effects on the moral, mental, and physical welfare of its rider; "wheel-riding" was, therefore, a topic that warranted a thorough debate at a medical conference in 1898. One of the participants, Doctor Libbie Hamilton-Muncie, argued that the medical practitioner, as "the conserver of public health," had to be prepared to offer advice to those parents whose children wanted to engage in new forms of recreation. When used properly, the bicycle was seen as having immense value as "the rider returns with renewed energies, courage, and hope, tears replaced by laughter and eyes sparkling with good nature." (I sent my brood out for a quick pedal around the block after I read this. It doesn't work.) N. G. Bacon shared this enthusiasm for wheel-riding. As Honorary Secretary of the Mowbray House Cycling Association she was a recognized authority on the subject and contributed a series of articles to *G.O.P.* on topics such as how to choose a bicycle and maintain it in first-rate running order. Her endorsement was unqualified: "The pastime of cycling is one of the most fascinating, health-giving, and educating for our girls." As for the connection between cycling and education, Mrs. Bacon pointed out that the newly acquired ability to explore the surrounding towns and countryside afforded the young person the opportunity to appreciate both geography and history.

But if used incorrectly, there were hazards. Doctor Weirick spoke on the issue of posture. The body was supposed to stay as erect as possible and the cyclist's tendency to lean forward and crouch over the handlebars made him very worried. He pointed out to the audience that professional rowers were known to have "derangement of the heart" because of their practice of bending forward repeatedly. He went on to debate whether or not the damage was more to the respiratory or the circulatory system; either way, you were likely to jeopardize your health and the racing posture adopted by today's top cyclists would have met with dire warnings.

There were also unspeakable consequences that could fall upon the unwitting cyclist. The crux of the matter was the saddle. When considering the impact of bicycle riding on girls, the image of a saddle between the legs was simply too much for some of the experts. A number argued that the bicycle could lead to impure thoughts, evil habits, and equally as evil behavior. Others were less convinced, citing as evidence that the proportion of prostitutes riding bicycles was no higher than that using public transportation. (I have never been able to determine if they actually conducted research to support this statement.) To be safe, Hamilton-Muncie urged mothers to make absolutely sure that the saddle and its rider were not too intimate, although she did not offer any specific suggestions as to how this might be accomplished. Perhaps girls of good family rode their bicycles standing up.

But What Do We Do On a Rainy Day?

Children obviously did not have the wealth of activities in the home that is available today. My youngest children could not imagine life without a vcr and I can only barely remember the early years before my parents could afford a television (perhaps the memories are too painful to recall.) The range of toys and games was also much narrower, as was the amount of disposable income needed for their purchase. For many writers, reading was a favored pursuit, but books can rarely get you through a whole day with a potentially bored and restless child. Chavasse considered music a respectable diversion, with the flute and bugle being highly praised for their beneficial effects on the lungs. Mrs. A. J. Graves, respected author of *Woman in America,* was not so sure, however, especially when its potential to undermine the modesty of young girls was remembered. Together with embroidery and dancing, music was too often put on show for family and friends and could fuel the child's "love of admiration and display." The Noah's ark deserves a special mention. Its enduring popularity was partly the result of its Biblical roots. While most toys had to be secured in the closet on Sundays, the ark was an acceptable diversion as it was in keeping with the spirit of the Sabbath. Hobbies such as painting and collecting became popular, as did games. Goss, who was obviously speaking from the heart, was ready to "lay a garland on the tombs or the heads of all dead or living inventors of good games for children." He applauded those humble geniuses who first constructed a top, a hobby-horse, a doll, a bagatelle board, jackstraws, ping-pong, and even tiddle-tewinks (the precursor of tiddly-winks.) He considered the inventors to be worthy of much praise and gratitude "for have they not kept the devil from finding mischief for idle hands?"

Board games constituted an expanding sector of the booming recreational industry. Educational themes were prominent; as has persisted into modern times, a number of companies sold their products by appealing to both children's wish to have fun and the parents' hope to increase their knowledge. Board games were created to teach vocabulary, history, and astronomy. Some also had a moral theme; the roll of a die could set you on a ladder to success or confront you with the serpent that awaited those who landed on one of the vices.

Fads and fashions came and went. For a while no child could hold her head up if she did not possess a toy theater boasting a cast of cardboard, cut-out figures (plain if you were of modest means; made of colored paper if you were wealthier). Dolls were the toy of choice for girls. They were, in fact, seen as a very valuable part of child-rearing. Although Chavasse was quite progressive in his encouragement of removing gender differences in play, he would not have approved of the girl who showed no interest in the more traditional activities. He reminded parents that dolls "teach a girl many valuable lessons and are a preparation for her woman's role." Although this notion may seem outdated, it has its advocates today. There is, for example, a widely read clinician who recommends asking mothers about their history of play during the course of custody assessments. The assumption is that playing with dolls in childhood is one sign of maternal leanings.

Dolls were also educational. Nowadays Barbie and her cousins arrive fully clothed and have a wide array of costumes and outfits that can be added to their wardrobes. Little girls in Victorian times, however, were expected to take on the task of providing their dolls with most of their

From mother to daughter: learning to sew a fine seam.

clothes. What might be given as a toy became a vehicle for teaching the sewing skills that were an important part of every girl's education.

Boys could also be educated through play. Toy soldiers were as much part of the boys' world of play as dolls were in the girls', and they reinforced society's view that a strong nation depended on its army of men to protect its interests. Complaints about "war toys" appear to have been rare; those that were made almost certainly reflected the minority opinion. A British book, *Management of Infants,* made mention of their power to "encourage warlike and savage propensities," and argued that the French were the worst when it came to giving such toys to their children. The writer suggested that this national shortcoming had "nourished a love of war in our neighbours." Notwithstanding the lack of historical evidence that the British were the doves and pacifists of the era, it seems dubious that the notion that war toys might influence attitudes or behavior would have been seen by most parents as grounds for removing them from the shelves.

Mechanical toys taught the scientific principles which were also considered to be part of the masculine world. One example I particularly like from Christina Hardyment's book *Dream Babies* is the pea-shooter as a means of demonstrating the principles of compressed air. Whether or not that argument was ever used successfully by a Victorian schoolboy after a successful, but observed attack on a fellow classmate is unknown.

Every so often a form of recreation came along that upset the experts greatly. I have already mentioned the evils of the common marble. Then there were playing cards, which Goss condemned as "a source of so much misery and crime." Their power to corrupt mystified the professionals. "What ingredient is mixed with that paper? What chemical is there in those paints? What spell or incantation was breathed over them by their inventor?" Reluctantly, he conceded that playing cards were here to stay, so better to teach them to play fish at home than have them sneak off to the loft or barn and get into a heavy-duty poker game.

Heralding the advent of electronic mass communication, the impact of the telephone received a special mention from the late Victorian commentators on children's indoor activities. With impressive acumen, they recognized that the unrestrained teenager would have a symbiotic relationship with the receiver and spend countless hours in conversations about the minutiae of their own and everyone else's lives. As one writer to a magazine was informed: "Naturally, the constant use of the telephone is injurious, creating aural over-pressure." When the advice-givers made statements of this nature, you could be sure that reference to evil was to follow. The "evil results" courted by the young person given to idling away her time on the telephone were overstimulation of the ear, nervous excitability, giddiness, and neuralgic pains. Based on this information, we have prepared warning signs to be displayed prominently by the phones in the house when our younger children reach their teens.

If space and money permitted, families had a separate nursery that would be decorated and equipped for the children. Wallpaper was fashionable and could be used to brighten up the room. Parents were warned, however, to exercise extreme caution when it came to such decoration, as some papers contained chemicals so toxic that four children in a single family had perished. The pictures on the walls would probably have a moral or religious message. "A fine engraving and a good painting elevate the mind," wrote Doctor Thomas Bull in 1840. Big Bird or Barney posters would simply not have cut it; early impressions were very important, as they helped purify the mind and keep the child from low company.

The nursery would contain space for books and toys and the children *always* tidied up after themselves. How the parents managed this is beyond my comprehension, but Hardyment provides a delightful quote on the topic. She mentions a prominent writer at the time, Mrs. Warren. In recalling her own childhood, Mrs. Warren describes how she often reminded her playmates that "Mamma likes to see the room tidy; let us all help to make it so." You might think that's too good to be true, but wait until you hear what followed. I would have predicted a "forget it" or "I didn't make any of this mess, so why should I clean it up?" from the other kids. Not so. "Then the little feet pattered about and the little hands were ready to be useful; then a kiss was given to each, and such a joyful clapping and shouting at the end of our labor." The only part that has any resemblance to what happens in our basement at the end of a rainy day is the shouting.

The Science of Play

For some, play was rooted in far more than a natural joyfulness. Science and theory combined to elevate play to unheard-of heights. This was particularly so during the latter Victorian period when the Child Study Movement was gaining ground. Dr. Stanley Hall, one of the founding members, was a prominent psychologist who was particularly renowned for his research into child and adolescent development. Drawing on theories regarding evolution and genetics, he argued that play was an expression of the impulses and behavior patterns that had been instrumental in the survival and development of the human species. In this context, children's running games paralleled the chasing and fleeing of primitive human hunting groups, while playing in the sand and mud was a reenactment of the time when the first life forms crawled onto the beaches. These instinctive urges had to be given an outlet. Although the rationale may be entirely different, this type of thinking reminds me of the permissive style of parenting that became so prevalent in the sixties. As a member of that particular generation, I know I tolerated a great deal more than I would now, all in the name of freedom of expression. I would probably have dismissed my two-year-old's flinging his plate of spaghetti across the room as a healthy release of emotion; for followers of Hall, however, this behavior would have literally been a modern version of hurling a spear at a woolly mammoth.

Encouraging and channeling play became very important matters. It was necessary to harness the power of the underlying instincts and direct them towards activities that would be adaptive and constructive in society. Play could be used to teach mastery and self-confidence. It could also be employed to teach the cooperation and loyalty needed to survive in the growing world of business and commerce. Playground associations flourished and were motivated, in part, by the concern that urbanization had reduced the opportunities for the types of physical pursuits that existed in rural environments.

Much of the thinking would find its proponents today. Many of us accept, for example, that involvement in team sports can help children develop a healthy balance between competition and cooperation. The term "team player" has also become a compliment, as it denotes someone who can make a substantial contribution while allowing others to do the same. But the Victorian experts on play went much further. It was proposed – and often taken as a matter of truth – that there was a direct link between play and the development of moral and social thinking. In the heyday of biological theories of human behavior, emotions and thinking were not distinguished from physical processes. "A healthy mind and a healthy body" was the maxim, and play was available for achieving both goals. The child with poor coordination who failed to strengthen his musculature through play was in peril. Given my level of participation and success in the type of play advocated by Hall and others, I for one would have been written off as morally bankrupt by the age of ten.

Spoiled Rotten?

The growing affluence of the nineteenth-century middle class added to the number of families that had money available to spend on luxuries. Gift-giving on birthdays and other special occasions created a demand that was welcomed by the manufacturers of toys and games. The parents' ability to provide such material benefits for their children was, however, seen as a mixed blessing. The question raised was that of deciding when being generous crossed the line into overindulgence. This concern about "spoiling" children is an issue that is as current today as it was a hundred years ago.

Every year just before Christmas my wife and I vow to spend less on the children's presents. We complain that they get too much and appreciate too little. Sometimes it seems we are winning. Early in November we begin reading tales like *Little House on the Prairie* to the children, reminding them of how the heroine, Laura, had been overwhelmed with joy and gratitude on discovering that Santa had left not only a candy cane, but also her very own tin cup. Then comes the pre-Christmas advertising blitz. The appeal of a candy cane and a tin cup pales into insignificance in the face of a remote-controlled death-star or a doll that performs all manner of bodily functions – batteries not included.

The fact that the ad campaigns often overcome our resolve is evident from the collection of barely used toys that seems to grow year by year. We long for simpler times, when children's loving thanks could be purchased with a modest toy. So did the Victorians. Goss, who was typically more optimistic in his outlook, was aghast at the materialist attitude of the younger generation. Children were described as "gluttons and drunkards of pleasure" whose greed and insatiability had rendered them a "burden to themselves and a torment to others." Before they were hardly out of their pinafores and knickerbockers they had "drained the cup of pleasure to its dregs." Parents were reminded that all they had needed as youngsters were a top or a doll. Now their children were throwing away expensive toys like miniature steam engines, pianolas, and cooking stoves almost before the bill arrived from the store. The effects were said to be far-reaching: the children were destined to become selfish, egotistical, and offensive. They were also using up their potential for future happiness, for "little people who enjoy at the age of ten what belongs to the age of twenty are spending their capital instead of living on their interest."

The advice was to keep life simple and to resist the temptation to spoil children with the latest products of the booming toy industry. Somehow I doubt too many Victorian parents were able to heed this advice, however appealing it might have been. When next Christmas rolls around there will be some comfort in knowing that we are not the first generation of parents who have succumbed to pressure. Chances are that our children will be no more "spoiled" by the experience than were their counterparts throughout history, and we have decided to stop feeling guilty about the fact that there is still no tin cup to be found in the house.

4. Education

I HAVE A NUMBER of standard lectures that I deliver in one form or another to my children. There's the "you're part of this family too" lecture which is designed to encourage them to request more chores and household responsibilities. The fact that it has been delivered more times than I care to remember speaks to its effectiveness. But probably the most popular (on my part) is the "don't you know the value of an education" lecture. It's quite long and detailed and contains sections on such topics as respecting teachers, doing more than expected rather than less, and recognizing the need to develop good study habits if you want to have a hope of graduating from kindergarten.

I know I am far from alone in my efforts to impress on my children that education is of great potential benefit to them. Academic achievement is a value that is considered a high priority by most families. A significant part of my practice as a clinical psychologist also centers around concerns parents have regarding their children's progress at school.

The importance our society attaches to education is reflected in the fact that it is considered not only a right, but a duty. We have created institutions to provide education for children and we insist they attend for a minimum of at least a decade. Education is seen as so important that not just anyone is allowed to provide the service. To be a teacher you almost always have to be part of a licensed profession and are required to undergo specialized training before being let loose on students to shape their young minds and push back the frontiers of their ignorance.

School and Home

I do not pretend that I have offered any new insights with my comments regarding the role of education. Everything I have said is obvious. What I find interesting, however, is that what is obvious today would not have been so in the early part of the last century. The practice of sending children to school to learn, for example, is relatively new in the history of the family. In the period leading up to the Victorian era the expectation was that children could often learn what they needed directly from their parents. Sometimes there was not too much that had to be learned. Being a goose-girl or a bird-scarer in England did not require extensive training. If the family earned its living from making clothes or growing produce, the skills needed might be more involved, but parents would be the most available and qualified instructors.

This type of family learning remained strong in Victorian times. Laura Ingalls Wilder's stories of growing up in a pioneer family in the latter part of the nineteenth century provides a particularly entertaining account of how the essential skills for survival and progress were handed down from parents to children in North America. Following Laura and her family from the woods of Wisconsin to the plains of Dakota gives the reader a crash course on curing ham, storing vegetables for the winter, building a log house, and making bullets.

For children during these periods of history, education was part and parcel of their upbringing. It was not until well into Victorian times that "education" referred primarily to the type of learning that took place in the school and consisted mainly of academic subjects.

Industrialization was one of the reasons for creating a school system. New and specialized skills were needed, as were higher levels of literacy. Increasingly fewer parents were seen as qualified to impart the type of knowledge required in society; the task of upbringing was, therefore, to be shared, with the state taking on a larger role in preparing children for the adult world.

Change is rarely smooth, and childcare experts joined in the fray that developed as attempts were made to establish a separate educational system. Some were highly critical of schools and recommended that, if more education were required than could be provided by the parents, private tutors should be hired whenever possible. The rigorous, if not cruel forms of discipline exercised by schoolteachers met with criticism and led one clergyman and politician in the early nineteenth century, Theodore Dwight, to declare, "school is a shock from which many bright children never recover." At the other extreme, parents who did not send their offspring to school might be warned that they would have to account to God for this grave neglect of duty. On their consciences would be the fact that their children would spend their miserable lives in a state of sin and stupidity and would be at a distinct disadvantage when called to account on Judgment Day. No excuse was acceptable. A pamphlet of the same era advised parents what they should do if a child tried to skip. After marching the offending child to the police station, they were to plead for the "privilege of his admission into the school for Juvenile Delinquency."

The fact that we now have an elaborate school system with compulsory attendance attests to the fact that the proponents of separating education from family life eventually prevailed. This transition, however, forced a number of issues to the forefront. If children were to participate in compulsory education, how much instruction should a child be given? When should this instruction begin? Should education be the same for girls and boys?

How Much Knowledge Is a Dangerous Thing?

I grew up in a school system that expected six hours' attendance, five days a week. By the time I was twelve, an average of two hours of homework a night was the expectation. More accurately, this was the teachers' expectation and one that few of us shared. But it would be safe to assume that we were stuck with a work week of at least thirty-five hours.

I cannot recall hearing a single sympathetic word from my parents regarding this deplorable state of affairs. No one commiserated with me when I complained that there was too much studying, and I found no support when I presented what I thought was a most convincing argument that I was being robbed of my childhood. Had I been born a hundred years previously, however, there would have been no shortage of child-care experts to champion my cause and join the picket line as we fought for a shorter work week and no compulsory overtime. I would have been able to muster a broad range of opinions to strengthen my case. A good opener would have been that too much formal education could lead to insanity. To back up my claims I could pull out my copy of *The Atlantic Magazine* from 1859 and present the case study of a child who died "insane from sheer overwork and raving of algebra" and remind them that no less than Doctor Chavasse declared that "the overworked, precocious brain is apt to cause the death of its owner." I would argue that, even if I managed to escape the jaws of death, school was definitely hazardous to both my mental and physical health. I would quote further from Chavasse, reminding them that overtaxing the brain of the student could "make an idiot of him." As for my physical well-being, I would have recourse to the body of knowledge establishing that having to memorize my times tables, as well as lengthy sections from *Hiawatha*, required the type of prolonged brain-work that was potentially debilitating. Such abuse would render me more prone to disease and lessen my ability to recuperate from illness. At this point I would cite Dr. Rankin's dire warning regarding the dangers of too much education: "If the life of the child be spared, the future is liable to be blighted by a general want of strength and by disorders caused by a defective nerve-force."

The advice to the Victorian parent was to watch children closely for the early signs that their brains were being overtaxed. These signs included a pallid countenance, frontal headache, puny, unhealthy looks, and defective digestion. What power would have been mine! All it would have taken was a complaint of indigestion following my morning porridge and I would have had the rest of the week off, as the prescribed remedy was an immediate reduction in the amount of schoolwork. Another danger signal was a fretful, irritable disposition. Given my temperament as an adolescent, I would have been on a permanent vacation from the age of twelve.

As for homework, my argument that I was being robbed of my childhood would have had its supporters. "To rob a child of the play time which belongs to him is a rank injustice." Hear, hear!

Setting the Pace

Another aspect of the advice regarding education was to tailor its pace according to the child's needs. Knowledge should be imparted when, and only when, it was actually needed. I had always known that conjugating Latin verbs was not preparing me for the world outside, and the chances of finding a sympathetic ear might have been much greater during the period when the value of education was being questioned and examined rather than assumed.

The Victorian ambivalence regarding education related to all ages. Kindergartens became increasingly popular, and their advocates showed no restraint in the claims they made regarding the benefits of early education. Having minds to shape and sculpt while they were still very young and pliable would, they argued, be a way to virtually eliminate crime and ensure that the person was on the path to salvation. The whole of society would gain through the creation of a generation of young people who had been brought up with the right values, interests, and skills. In this way, early involvement in regulated forms of education was seen by some as a desirable and effective form of social engineering.

The opposing viewpoint emphasized caution: children needed to develop slowly. It would be damaging to try to "develop the flower before the stalk is grown," wrote H. N. Hudson. Writing in the *Democratic Review* in 1845, he advocated a more patient approach: "The mental facilities should be allowed to develop slowly, as much as possible without stimulation, and the life of a child should be more like that of a young animal." It was argued that children under six "will absorb ideas as rapidly as it is good for the brain simply from association with older people." Another argument against early education related primarily to theories of muscle development. It was asserted that the child's finger muscles did not mature sufficiently until the eighth or ninth year of life. Before then, children's lack of dexterity precluded such activities as writing, and forcing them to do so would be ineffective or damaging. Phrenology also had an impact.

Its notion that abilities could not emerge until the necessary brain structures had developed added weight to the view that book-learning should not be introduced too soon in the child's life.

Chavasse allowed for more deliberate efforts to instruct the child, but wanted learning to occur through "a course in education in play." The curriculum should be no more formal than hearing stories on the mother's knee, singing songs, and being exposed to nature in the course of daily outdoor play. No regular lessons should start until the age of seven and he heaped scorn on those who advocated half-day school for five-year-olds: "If this be not slavery, what is it?" This belief that the trend towards earlier formal education was injurious was often accompanied by the recommendation that only older children should attend for a full day. The seven-year-old could be enrolled in school, but a maximum of three and a half hours of instruction a day might be maintained until the age of ten.

Reading, Writing, and Arithmetic

Wars could almost be started over the content of the school curriculum and the method of teaching it. There are those who would like to go "back to basics" and see the learning centers that dominate primary classrooms today replaced by neat rows of desks. Their concern is that too much emphasis is placed on creativity and making learning "fun." While not necessarily miserable and authoritarian by nature, these parents and educators also argue for an acceptance of the reality that hard work, persistence, and drill are essential ingredients of the learning process. This debate is not new: an identical view was held by a number of Victorian experts. They deplored what they saw as a lowering of academic standards in schools. To their mind, students were being catered to, coddled, and conned into believing that everything in life should be interesting, enjoyable, and relaxed; the generation of spoon-fed students that was being created would expect too much and give too little.

Given the increasing importance of literacy in the nineteenth century, no one disagreed that reading and writing should be core subjects. Math also occupied an undisputed position in the curriculum. Beyond these areas of learning, however, the value of particular branches of knowledge could easily be questioned. The more conservative educators argued that the core curriculum described above was all that was needed. Moreover, this curriculum could be applied throughout the child's schooling with only modifications for age levels being necessary. Suggestions from the reformers that music and nature would not only brighten, but also enrich the student's day were met with cynicism and outright resistance. Rather than being seen as encouraging self-expression and creativity, art was more likely to be viewed as a sign of lack of discipline.

The Victorians also debated the merit of departing from the core curriculum to teach practical subjects that could help the student find a trade or acquire domestic skills. As theories regarding the practice of education were developed, this debate became more complex, and some educators challenged the distinction between academic and vocational skills. A woodworking project could be a vehicle for learning about almost anything. It required math to build according to specifications and language skills to read the specifications in the first place. The creative teacher could go on to introduce geography (where does the lumber come from?). There were plenty of songs about lumberjacks and log rollers, so a musical interlude could be added.

Girls and Boys

The assumption that boys were destined to work outside the home made them obvious candidates for an educational system that could prepare them for competitive employment. But girls were a different story. The assumption that their destiny centered on hearth and home may have been challenged in some quarters, but it was firmly engrained in the culture at large.

Gender role stereotyping had a strong impact on the expectations for female students. First of all, experts argued that girls were short more than a few neurons when it came to higher learning. Furthermore, they were apt to have little interest in utilizing the limited mental power they did possess. "Young women are unwilling to think," wrote Doctor Alcott in the *Gift Book For Young Ladies,* and added, "hence the importance of their being frequently and earnestly admonished."

Although smart enough to write *The Daughters of England* in the early Victorian era, Sara Ellis subscribed to this view of the female capacity to learn and achieve. "As women then, the first thing of importance is to be content to be inferior to men – inferior in mental power in the same proportion as you are inferior in body strength." Emphasis was to be placed on preparing girls for their domestic roles. Their primary goal – and for some writers the necessary condition for successful adulthood – was to ensure that they became wives and mothers. In this context, the value of formal education for girls was scrutinized carefully. The extreme position that schooling was a threat to the feminine ideal of refinement and delicacy was reflected in John Gregory's *A Father's Legacy to His Daughters*. The book was popular in the early part of the nineteenth century and conveyed the message that girls and women were to be silent in company. Quick retorts and witty one-liners were out, as such humor would be an "enemy to delicacy." If you had managed to learn anything that had more depth than knowing the best way to get rid of ring-around-the-collar, you were to keep it to yourself: "If you happen to have any learning, keep it a profound secret, especially from men" was the advice.

For the more enlightened, however, the emphasis on gender roles did not have to mean that girls were destined to become no more than illiterate skivvies. No man would want to come home to a wife whose horizons did not extend beyond cooking, cleaning, and laundry. Although these activities might indeed occupy most of her day, the woman should at least know something of the broader world from which she was excluded. There was, therefore, an agreement that girls should be schooled. Literature and the arts were appropriate and a smattering of history and geography would not hurt. But technical subjects and the sciences were a different matter. These had no relevance to performing domestic duties and were, in any case, too complex for the female mind.

The theorists at the time were quick to justify the separation of the genders. Girls were made differently; their innate differences were a fact of life and no one should mess with Nature's design. If this line of reasoning did not leave you totally convinced, you were reminded that the Virgin Mary, who would be the undisputed role model for any girl, "knew nothing of letters." The fact that Joseph might not have scored that well on tests of reading or spelling was conveniently ignored.

For many Victorian advice-givers, the onset of puberty was the time to ensure that gender role training was undertaken with renewed vigor. As physical differentiation became more pronounced, so did the awareness that girls and boys were supposed to be headed in different directions. The Laws of Nature were indisputable – too much education of the mind would be at the expense of the body. Rankin presented a case study of a fourteen-year-old girl who collapsed at a party and remained in a state of exhaustion for weeks. She had been a child who had a thirst for knowledge and this had been her downfall. The "unnatural strain" of learning had induced a physical and mental breakdown. By overstimulating her brain she had denied her rapidly changing reproductive organs the energy needed to develop. The cure was straightforward: no studies whatsoever for a year and then only "light mental work" was permitted.

If the threat of social failure and physical collapse during puberty were insufficient deterrents, the prospect of what awaited the young woman who insisted on pursuing higher education must have been daunting. The mainstay of the biological argument continued to be the conflicting needs of the brain and reproductive system. Towards the end of the Victorian era, Doctor Edward Clarke wrote extensively on the topic of women's inherently weaker constitutions and stated in no uncertain terms that higher education could cause the uterus to atrophy. Another authority, Doctor Coleman, commenting on how the evils of corsets had been supplanted by the evils of education, stated "Women beware. You are on the brink of destruction. You have hitherto been engaged in crushing your waists; now you are attempting to cultivate your mind." He went on to talk about the dangers of wrestling with Euclid while the body slowly degenerated.

Once on a roll, the Victorian expert knew no bounds. The atrophy of the uterus could be followed by loss of mammary function. Not only could the breasts cease to be operational, they might also shrink and even disappear. Using this logic, a daily diet of problems in Euclidian geometry could become the safest form of breast reduction yet discovered.

If fear of physical damage did not suffice, then fear of insanity could be evoked. Proof was offered: women in asylums were more likely to be educated than were male patients; the brainwork had simply been too much for their feeble minds.

Guilt was another powerful weapon used by the Victorians. Sacrificing the reproductive system in a vain pursuit of knowledge was selfishness of the first degree. Women were reminded that they had been charged with the responsibility of producing healthy members of the next generation. They had the solemn duty of passing along all those genetic predispositions that mankind had struggled to perfect. If they turned away from their God-given role, then the whole human race was threatened, if not doomed.

In the face of the arguments used to maintain gender role stereotyping, it was inevitable that the movement towards equal opportunity for girls in the educational system became a prolonged and arduous struggle. No one disputed the role of the biological distinctions between the genders; what was criticized by early feminists, however, was the prejudice and pigeon-holing that accompanied them. As Professor Emily Davies remarked in 1866, "It is not against the recognition of real distinction, but against arbitrary judgements not based on reason that the protest is made." This protest continues to be necessary; more than a century after this statement, researchers continue to find that, although the techniques might be more subtle, boys in elementary school receive more reinforcement for learning than girls. At the high-school level, girls' achievement decreases, especially in the sciences, and only very recently have young women demonstrated that they can easily hold their own in fields such as engineering – and even retain their figures and fertility.

5. Health

MRS. SIGOURNEY was a poet and author whose works were read widely in the latter half of the eighteenth century. Her poetry, in particular, is a powerful reminder of how vulnerable children were before the advent of modern medicine. Her work, *Poems for Their Mothers*, appears almost morbid because of its repeated references to dying children and heartbroken parents. The fact that nearly a third of her poems dealt with these topics, however, reflected the reality of her times rather than any preoccupation with the somber and morose. *Departed Little Ones* speaks of how parents' deep attachments to their children exposed them to the risk of experiencing the type of loss that most of us fear and dread:

> Forth as the buds of spring they come,
> Around our hearts they twine,
> With all their growing, winning charms,
> Like tendrils of the vine.
> Yet oft, while in their cloudless joy,

They feel the morning ray,
And feed upon the dews of love,
They fleet like dews away.

The death of a child remained a common tragedy for families throughout the Victorian era. Diseases were poorly understood and knowledge regarding their transmission was limited. Treatments were often ineffective or were themselves as dangerous as the ailments they were supposed to alleviate or cure. Parents were forced to watch their children suffer, and suffer to the point where death was almost a welcome relief. Sigourney again portrayed this sad reality in her account of a boy dying in pain. In

The impending death of a child: a common tragedy for Victorian families.

the final scene, his mother is striving to comfort her son with his favorite hymn: "And as she controlled her grief that she might lull his death-pangs with the hymn he loved, he fondly laid his lamb-like head upon her shoulder and murmured his last, low tones – 'Come, mamma, let us go to sleep.' And he slept in Jesus."

As standards of hygiene and nutrition increased, so did the health of the general population, but these changes were slow and issues relating to infant mortality continued to be addressed in many childcare books published towards the end of the century. The fear of illness and disease must have motivated many parents to seek any advice available regarding how to increase the chances of having a healthy child who would survive to see adulthood. As a result, many aspects of day-to-day care, such as diet, hygiene, and exercise, assumed great importance. The experts did not present options; they insisted that the consequences of ignoring their advice would be serious, if not lethal.

The Womanly Art of Breast-feeding?

One of the most enduring controversies in the field of infant nutrition has been breast-feeding. The fact that it has been an essential and effective aspect of survival among mammals for countless millennia has not meant that it has always been deemed acceptable by the Establishment. Its opponents were vocal at various points throughout the last century. Some used imagery in an effort to persuade mothers that breast-feeding was about as far removed from their cherished goals of gentility and delicacy as one could ever get. "Let no mother condemn herself to be a common or ordinary cow," came the plea from Mrs. Patton's late Victorian baby care manual. Such advice capitalized on the view that those women who occupied the middle and upper classes were at the pinnacle of evolutionary development and should not act like lowly beasts of the field. This was a far cry from the days when babies might be suckled by a goat or donkey if the mother's milk was not forthcoming. The distaste for breast-feeding also reflected very different attitudes from those underlying the practice of hiring the services of a wet-nurse. For the opponents of breast-feeding, a cow was a cow whether it was a member of the family or just rented.

The idea that nursing was a crude and vulgar practice was reinforced by the expectation that it had to be conducted in private. Special garments and apparatus were also designed that would allow a tube to run directly from the nipple, through the clothing, and to the baby.

The use of negative imagery and social stigma was supplemented by suspect biological theories. It was argued that the women of the middle and upper classes, although becoming increasingly refined, were less robust than had been the case in harsher times. Breast-feeding would, therefore, place the mother at risk of complete physical collapse. A specific caution was that, being in such a weakened condition, she would be prey to alcoholism.

There have been numerous facets to the discussion of why the anti-breast-feeding movement was strong. Some of the underlying reasoning may have been benign, although clearly incorrect when viewed with the wisdom of hindsight. With the discovery of pasteurization, cow's milk was deemed particularly desirable as its safety was guaranteed. Food technology was also advancing rapidly and the development of baby foods carried with it the potential to offer a balanced and healthy diet to the infant. The undisputed queen of the kitchen, Mrs. Beeton added her support to the theory that prepared food was superior to nursing. The child, she maintained, would be stronger and less liable to infectious diseases. She gently reminded mothers of the high stakes involved, making reference to numerous children who could have avoided serious illnesses or faulty development had they received a diet that consisted largely or wholly of prepared foods.

Others argued that less severe, but still negative consequences could occur through biological mechanisms. Exertion or excitement of the passions on the nursing mother's part would affect the milk in such a way that the infant would be liable to have convulsions. To avoid such risk to the baby, the mother would have to refrain from all forms of strenuous activity, while her non-nursing counterpart was free to dance, play tennis, and get passionate once in a while.

The genuineness of the desire to provide better infant care is not questioned. The irony, however, was that evoking fears of illness and disease led to practices that were to heighten, rather than reduce, health risks. We now know that early breast-feeding typically strengthens the baby's immune system and that, for most infants, nursing provides an excellent and sufficient diet. The move to infant formula not only deprived babies of this early form of protection, it also exposed them to infection through use of feeding bottles and other devices that were inadequately cleaned and sterilized.

The importance many Victorian writers attached to strict routines and regimens also had relevance for mothers who were deciding how to feed their babies. Advice that the newborn child should adhere to a rigid schedule with up to four hours between feedings would not have been uncommon. Such a regimen, you were told, was an excellent opportunity to foster self-discipline and obedience in your offspring. Demand-feeding, on the other hand, would sow the seeds of self-indulgence. If you accepted this advice, the chances of having a baby who did not scream and cry for a sizeable portion of the day would be minimal had you opted for breast-feeding.

The emphasis on feeding schedules may have been at least partially the result of practices that were of convenience to those employed in hospitals or institutions that catered to children. The writers of baby books were often employed in the health care or social service sectors and demand-feeding would have been incompatible with the goal of establishing a well-ordered and controlled children's ward or orphanage. Another argument was that breast-feeding gave women too much prominence and power in child-rearing and threatened male domination of the family.

Other factors apart from concern for child welfare may have influenced people to speak against breast-feeding. The sexual connotations were probably too distressing for some Victorians. Nursing required at least temporary, partial nudity and in a sexually repressive culture, modesty must be presented as the correct image, even if not actually practiced. Wielding a spoon or baby bottle could, in principle, be done by either gender and could be performed in public without embarrassment. Baring the breast was an entirely different matter.

There was also a great deal of money to be earned from developing special foods for infants. It was good marketing sense, therefore, to create an image of a healthy, rosy-cheeked baby with her face lit up as she sees a spoonful of New Formula Gruel heading her way. Such an image had even more power when contrasted with the picture of the nursing mother as a grazing cow.

But the Victorian times were full of extremes. For some experts the fact that nursing was a natural, mammalian practice rendered it desirable rather than unbecoming. For the baby, the breast was a birthright, not an inferior or dangerous method of feeding. Doctor Chavasse was a staunch supporter of such views and, unless illness prevented nursing, had a low opinion of the mother who would deny her infant this basic right: "It is most unnatural and very cruel for her not to suckle her child," was a consistent message throughout his lengthy and detailed discussion of the merits and practice of breast-feeding. I suspect that one reason for his popularity was his attention to detail. It often seems as if he were writing especially for the first-time mother who, however educated and intelligent she might be, was probably feeling ill-equipped to deal with the task of caring for a helpless, needy, and demanding baby. Chavasse spelled everything out. He talked explicitly about preparing for breast-feeding and described techniques for getting the infant on the right track. His cautions about diet during nursing were accompanied by an extensive list of foods that were suitable and those that should be avoided. He encouraged mothers to be patient if their milk was slow to come and urged them to pay attention to their comfort and well-being. If the breasts became engorged, he recommended plenty of rest and applications of young cabbage leaves. Another remedy was to engage the services of a "suck-pap" who, for a modest sum, would suck the excess milk from the painful breasts. Only the "head of her profession" should be employed, however, to ensure that she was clean, sober, healthy, and respectable.

While Chavasse agreed that strenuous exercise would "disorder the milk," he proposed a simple solution: take it easy and limit aerobics to daily constitutionals in the fresh air. The fact that dancing was out for the nursing mother was also a plus; the woman who frequented ballrooms was as much an anathema to Chavasse as the mother who chose the bottle or wet-nurse.

The argument that bottle-feeding was more conducive to the early training and discipline of the child was similarly dismissed by Chavasse. Mothers were told to establish a schedule so that the baby would acquire good habits and learn that he could not expect to be indulged in life. Within the first few months, a four-hourly regimen was to be in place – no exceptions.

Just as the opponents of nursing had argued that breast milk could pass on negative influences from the mother, its advocates suggested that the opposite was true. The virtuous and moral mother could expect to begin at least partial transmission of her laudable qualities through nursing. The mother given to good temper and reasonableness would also produce wholesome milk, thereby raising a wholesome child who would join the ranks of the good-tempered and reasonable. She also had nothing to fear when it came to her own physical welfare. In fact, she was informed that she would enjoy better physical health than the non-nursing mother and be more attractive to boot.

Wet-nursing was only to be considered if all efforts to suckle had failed. The problem was that, once it was decided that certain qualities were transmitted via breast milk, it became critical to ensure that the source was as pristine as possible. It went without saying that the wet-nurse should be of good moral character. She should also be willing to have her life and daily activities subjected to a level of scrutiny and control that would incite mutiny among self-respecting employees today. Guidelines were given for the exercise schedule that should be followed; an indolent and sluggardly wet-nurse would be a potential hazard to the infant. Her diet was to be regulated carefully. For breakfast, Chavasse recommended black tea with perhaps a slice or two of cold meat. Should the ravenous wet-nurse feel faint by eleven o'clock, a "tumbler of porter or mild fresh ale with a piece of dry toast soaked in it" would help her make it through to her lunch of meat and vegetables, washed down with more ale. By now I suspect nurse was feeling more than pleased with her chosen career as she gazed down at the equally as content and beaming baby. By the time she consumed the porter or ale that accompanied supper, I doubt that she cared much about the rest of the menu, which was fortunate, as Chavasse liked wet-nurses to finish the day with a large bowl of gruel.

The question of weaning became an issue of debate among the supporters of breast-feeding. Assumptions abounded. Weaning too soon was dangerous, but so was prolonging nursing. Some adopted the maxim, "carry for nine, and suckle for nine," but there was far from consensus among the experts on this issue. They did agree, however, that untimely weaning could lead to dire consequences for all concerned. The baby denied her full quota of breast milk would lose muscular strength and become delicate and sickly. Too much milk and she would also be delicate, as well as flabby. As for the mother, late weaning was given as a cause of deafness, blindness, emaciation, hysteria, and consumption (tuberculosis).

The forces that dampened enthusiasm for breast-feeding, however, remained powerful and continued to have an effect well into the twentieth century. When my first child was born in the sixties, breast-feeding would have been acceptable, but the bottle seemed the more obvious choice for us and many of our generation of young parents. My last child was born in the late eighties and by that time breast-feeding seemed finally to have the status it deserved as a viable choice.

Candies, Cakes, and Cookies

According to the advice given to Victorian parents I should have been institutionalized for moral degeneracy years ago. We of British origin are, in my opinion, much slandered when it comes to our culinary tastes and abilities. I defy anyone to top the delights of bread and dripping (sprinkled liberally with salt) or a chip-buttie. (For the gastronomically deprived, a chip-buttie is a white-bread sandwich that contains hot french fries. A thick layer of butter is essential; the taste buds will reach indescribable heights of ecstasy as the butter melts and mingles with the hot fries.) Then there is the English afternoon tea. My friends and I grew up in spite of our fare of little cakes, assorted cookies, and on special occasions, scones with clotted cream.

I am forced to concede that the above delicacies lack nutritional soundness and I have finally joined the ranks of those who attempt to convince themselves that beginning the day with a bowl of bran and a cup of herbal tea actually beats a coffee and Danish. But such changes would have been far too late in the Victorian era; my early dietary habits would have set me on a path of physical or moral decline. A recurrent theme in the childcare literature was that certain foods would have the effect of overstimulating the body. Desserts and candy were considered particularly hazardous materials; Doctor Rankin decreed that jam, for example, "causes indigestion, distends the bowels with wind, and disturbs the whole circulation, especially of the brain." The connection between sugar and dental decay was not understood, but the experts had no doubt in their minds of sugar's potential to excite tendencies and passions in children that were best left undisturbed. A popular argument was that sugary foods led to addictions. Horace Bushnell, a nineteenth-century theologian with a particular interest in child-rearing, pronounced that virtually all drunkenness was the result of "vicious feeding" by which children were taught to develop a taste for sweets and candies. For those of you who have difficulty accepting that your homemade lemon meringue pie places your children in moral jeopardy, let me explain why it threatens more than people's waistlines. Once a taste is developed for such food, the person becomes almost addicted to self-indulgence. For Bushnell, the connection was indisputable, and he claimed that many a young child "taken by the captivating flavor of some dainty or confectionery has refused to restrain itself."

Even worse than the confectionery itself was the practice of using such treats to pacify or control children. At this point I have to confess my own guilt. As a parent I am aware of the awesome power that is mine whenever I wave a pack of gum in front of my noncompliant child; as a psychologist, I was brought up believing that the M & M is one of the most effective socialization agents known. According to Bushnell, however, I was helping to create the next generation of antisocial adults, as using candy as a reward can transform the child into an "ill-natured, morbid sensualist, and feigning cheat."

Doctor Alcott went as far as to depict the candy store as nothing short of a house of ill repute. His book, *The Young Mother,* was available throughout the early and mid-Victorian times and he was adamant that such establishments should be given a wide berth. The child would inevitably come into contact with a bad crowd – presumably those older children whose penchant for chocolate bars had already eroded their moral fiber. It was only a short step from "these places of pollution to the grog shop, the gambling house, or the brothel."

Although the tirades against sweets and cakes seem excessive, there was a legitimate basis for at least some of the trepidation. Chavasse referred to cakes as a "slow poison," but not without reason. In 1858 the highly reputable medical journal, *The Lancet*, had published a report of the chemicals often contained in the manufacture of the artificial colorings used by confectioners. Among those listed were lead, copper, mercury, and arsenic. Chavasse's solution was to avoid sweets altogether and he pointed out that the child who had never tasted such forbidden fruit would never know what he was missing. As a substitute the mother could offer stale bread. His advice was quite specific and it was apparent that he viewed bread much like a wine that needed time to mature and blossom. It was to be two to three days old in the summer; a week old in the winter. When so eaten at its prime, the child "will consider a piece of dry bread a luxury and will eat it with the greatest relish."

Pickles, pepper, and spices were other threats to the child's moral integrity. Kellogg and Rankin both wrote extensively on their evils. They would create a desire for highly seasoned food, which Rankin stated "leads in turn directly to intemperance in later life." Once again, the Victorian concern regarding drunkenness surfaced, and probably for very understandable reasons given the incidence of alcoholism among adults and children. But connecting early food preferences to later substance abuse relied on presenting what was no more than an assumption as a proven fact – namely, that the child who could be satisfied with a pure and wholesome diet would remain content with a lifestyle that was equally as pure and wholesome.

Opinions differed when it came to meat-eating. Some argued that, once beyond infancy, the child needed to be a confirmed carnivore if he were to become a strong and courageous adult. As proof, it was claimed that all courageous animals were carnivores (the dietary habits of the rhinoceros, moose, and gorilla were overlooked). It was also a good idea to start the day with a good helping of meat and the hearty breakfast could include mutton chops and cold game. Others disagreed. While meat was acceptable, the portions should be limited. Such advice might be given today, but not for the same reasons. In the nineteenth century those who opposed frequent meat-eating for children claimed that it led to coated tongues, foul breath, indigestion, and talking in their sleep. The child who only occasionally was treated to a modest helping of boiled mutton, however, could expect to have a healthier complexion and rosier cheeks. He would also be blessed with a generally happier, brighter disposition.

At times the net effect of Victorian opinions regarding nutrition was probably advantageous for children. For many authors, the staple items of the child's diet should include mild cereals (oatmeal boiled for three hours until it obtained a gelatinous appearance was a favorite), vegetables, and fruit. Not all recommended diets were bland, however, and if you had the right temperament as a child you might literally be wined and dined. Ada Ballin's views appeared regularly in the advice literature and her opinions regarding nutrition were based on a theory of innate personality traits. For example, she recommended coffee, tea, and even wine to give the system a boost when the child was of a sluggish and slow disposition. The more active youngster, on the other hand, was to receive nothing more exciting than foods such as milk and vegetables. Critics of the tendency to limit meals to standard, unimaginative fare could also be found. Variety, they said, was needed and parents should allow their children the opportunity to extend their gastronomic experiences beyond boiled oatmeal, boiled mutton, and boiled turnips.

Gender differences were a factor that had to be considered when planning children's diets. At Thanksgiving the properly delicate girl would not, for example, think of vying for a drumstick. She would request only white meat (but never breast). Particularly in adolescence she would be steered well away from "robust" food such as corned beef or blood pudding, whereas boys' physical prowess and competitive instincts allowed for such items to be on their menus.

The impact of education was an additional area to consider. One of the Victorian concerns about public schooling was that attendance would disrupt the mandatory schedule of regular and leisurely meals. For the under-tens, some writers recommended that classes end by noon so that the child could return home for lunch and have plenty of time afterwards for digestion. The habit of allowing older children money to buy a lunch was frowned upon, as they would be sure to use it to purchase tarts and cakes. Just as today, a nourishing packed lunch was to be provided, although I suspect the modern-day student might balk at the suggestion of a mutton sandwich and the yolk of a hard-boiled egg. The physician who recommended this menu, possibly aware that it might have lacked appeal, suggested taking the risk of including a little stale sponge cake as an incentive.

Discipline and diet were also closely associated in many writers' minds. Doctor Emmett Holt, who began writing about childcare at the end of the Victorian era, epitomized this viewpoint and I consider myself to be a victim of his continuing influence well into this century. I would wager large sums of money that the "lunch lady" who supervised our cafeteria at elementary school had been raised in a home where his manual was treated as gospel. She had the task of ensuring that the subsidized meals provided for children in postwar British schools were consumed with decorum and gratitude. One day we staged a revolt. No more would we eat the rehydrated mashed potato that was indistinguishable from the lumpy paste we used in art class. En masse we piled our plates and took them to the dish trolley. The lunch lady promptly and quietly returned the plates, peeled them apart, and sat one down in front of each activist without so much as an inkling of concern as to whose was whose. Not a word was spoken, but as we struggled to swallow the last of the lumps, we knew the rebellion was over.

Whatever our opinion of her might have been, she would have been hailed as a heroine by Holt and his colleagues. It was not simply a question of avoiding waste; finishing what was put in front of you had far-reaching implications. First of all, it was an indication of effective parental authority. Just as infants were supposed to feed according to a rigid schedule, so older children were to learn to eat what they were given at their prescribed meal times. Early compliance with this, as well as any other aspect of early upbringing, would breed self-control and respect for authority. Relax your expectations and the child would be ill-equipped to resist the temptations that awaited him in later life.

Predictably, premature death was another fate hanging over the heads of those who failed to follow the advice. The argument used was very similar to that put forward to underscore the need for automatic and blind obedience in children. If you did not learn to eat your spinach or rutabaga when called upon to do so, what would happen if you fell ill and had to take medicine? Chances were good you would accept an early transfer to the next life rather than open your mouth to the offending substance. When speaking of this possibility, Rankin brought to bear all the weight of his clinical experience: "I have known repeatedly cases where the lives of children, precious to their parents, could have been saved if the parents had exercised a little more judgement and had not only taught their children to eat proper kinds of food, but had enforced obedience in eating whatever was placed before them."

Bladders and Bowels

Towards the end of the Victorian era a group of physicians came together to form the Society of Orificial Surgeons. As the title suggests, they shared an interest in the functioning of body orifices. One of their major concerns was the high incidence of constipation and many of their papers discussed how surgical means could be employed to alleviate the problem. Devoting their professional lives to orifices would not have been considered strange in their time. Constipation had been an issue addressed by many childcare authorities and the daily bowel movement was seen as the cornerstone of health. "Many parents are not aware of the misery and discomfort, to say nothing of ill health, that they are responsible for by neglecting to impress upon the child the extreme necessity of a daily action from the bowels," wrote Rankin, who was as concerned about elimination as he was about ingestion. Although other writers expressed more tolerance for individual differences in how frequently a person received what were commonly referred to as the "calls of Nature," most appear to have assumed that anything less than a daily call was likely to be a problem.

Early training became an important goal for those who were convinced that constipation had to be avoided at all costs. The argument that bowel training was also an essential part of child-rearing has been discussed in the chapter on discipline and this argument was used to counter any suggestion that perhaps parents should wait until the infant or toddler seemed ready to use a potty or "water closet." Toilet training was no easy matter when applied to infants, but long before they were capable of sitting, babies were to be encouraged to relieve both their bowels and bladders by placing them on the chamber pot before, during, and after each meal. Parents were also advised to encourage a bowel movement by stimulating the rectum. Holt, for example, suggested "tickling the anus, or introducing just inside the rectum a small cone of oiled paper, or a piece of soap." Laxatives, including the castor oil that epitomized the Victorian weakness for foul-tasting home remedies, were recommended and appeared to have been used widely.

Constipation can obviously be a problem. Not all families would have either received or followed recommendations regarding inclusion of liberal quantities of vegetables, fruit, and fiber in children's diets and ways to increase regularity would have been sought by many parents. The functioning of the lower bowel – and by association, the bladder – became so prominent as potential concerns, however, that it is hardly surprising that they were to feature so strongly in Freud's theories of infant development and neuroses.

Constipation was also linked to mental effort. Doctor G. Durant Hood discussed this topic in detail at the turn of this century. He had apparently discovered a new form of writers' block; in *The Practical Family Physician* he revealed there are many authors who "seldom have their bowels relieved oftener than once a week." This led to the prescription of regular exercise. While such advice was commendable, wearing a bandage around the abdomen, avoiding a morning lie-in, the odd drop of laudanum (opium), and a change of scenery were recommendations that would have been either ineffective or harmful. On a more practical note, he spoke of the problems that could arise for the household that contained many occupants, but boasted only one bathroom. He encouraged parents to spend less of their money on the more decorative aspects of their homes or apartments and ensure that whenever the call came, there was at least a place to answer it.

Bedwetting was another behavior that alarmed the Victorians, and lack of bladder control in a child was linked to lack of control by the parents. Doctor Conquest was a family physician who had a particular interest in this problem. Writing in the early part of the nineteenth century, he stated that the problem was usually due to "deficient care and want of moral training." Several decades later, Hood referred to it as one of the most troublesome complaints suffered by children, and he told parents that "no effort should be spared to alleviate it." As a result, the discomfort of waking up in a wet bed could become minor in comparison to what lay

in store for the child. Having his body rubbed all over with a stiff brush
was one recommended treatment. This might be followed by a poultice
made from ground-up beetles that would be hot enough to cause a large
blister. At the other extreme of temperatures, spraying the genital area
with cold water was prescribed.

Cold Baths and Fresh Air

It is strange how certain trivia can become long-term memories. I grew up
in a society where the British monarchy was held in high regard and, as
children, we viewed the royal family with much awe and envy. I can recall,
however, the exact moment at which I no longer felt envy for my age peer,
Prince Charles. He had been sent to a boarding school in Scotland and we
read that his day always started with a cross-country run, followed by a
cold shower. I was suddenly overwhelmed by feelings of gratitude and relief that, as a mere commoner, my day could start with nothing more en-
ergetic or traumatic than walking downstairs to the breakfast table.

Charles's great-great-grandmother would no doubt have approved of
his daily rude awakening. The importance of fresh air was often discussed
in childcare literature and the fact that so many writers felt a need to give
such advice may have reflected the habit of keeping houses sealed tight because of fears of the "chills" and the belief that the nighttime air could be
hazardous to the health. Parents were advised that, provided the child was
suitably attired, windows were to be opened; a minimum of a daily walk
or "constitutional" was also prescribed. Rankin devoted a chapter to the
"importance of pure air" and many of his comments and beliefs would be
supported today. No one would argue, for example, with his emphasis on
ensuring adequate ventilation in the home. We might, however, question
his view that opening windows in the morning was essential to allow certain poisonous gases to exit. These gases were "thrown out through the
system through the lungs and from the surface of the body" and contained
a "poison of a virulent character." Apparently research had been conducted into this matter. Distilled vapor from human lungs had been in-
jected into a rabbit, who promptly died. This adds a whole new dimension
to morning breath and, if the research can be replicated, it would be in-
valuable to the promoters of mouthwashes.

Reading childcare manuals from the nineteenth century frequently provides reminders of how technology that would now go unnoticed had a major impact on family life when it was first developed. The perambulator, or baby carriage, is one such example. It was in mass production by

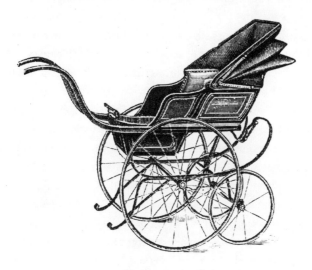

A "wretched perambulator."

the latter part of the century and the knowledge that Queen Victoria herself had acquired several for the royal children added to their popularity. The growing number of prams on the streets and sidewalks was not, however, met with universal approval in spite of the fact that it made the daily trips into the fresh air far easier to orchestrate for infants. Doctor Chavasse complained of how the drivers of "these wretched perambulators" were a menace to others because of their habit of looking in every direction except in front. He leaves the reader with an image of countless pedestrians either running for cover or lying on the ground nursing broken legs or bruised shins after a baby carriage has plowed through their midst. Other objections centered on the degree to which the baby might be shaken or bumped given the sorry state of many roads and pathways; if prams were to be used, several layers of padding were recommended. Writers also commented on how prams "distanced" infants from their mothers as there was no longer any need to hold the baby during a walk. Notwithstanding the nay-sayers, the perambulator and its descendants were to become commonplace and there was no excuse for not providing even the smallest child with the benefits of a daily dose of fresh air.

As a person who relishes a long, leisurely soak in a hot bath, I have a great deal of sympathy for the countless numbers of Victorian children who endured daily dousing with cold water. The enthusiasm for this practice was strong in the early part of the era and the advice included bathing infants in cold water for up to an hour. Accounts survive of children being brought out to the courtyard and confronted with a tub of water covered by a thin layer of ice. The addition of a dash of warm water might be condoned, but only for the very delicate child and only in the winter. Lack of cooperation and enthusiasm was anticipated, but the benefits were immense even if they were not immediately obvious to the child. As well as curing constipation, "thorough cold water ablutions banish all, or nearly all, of her little ailments and nervousness," wrote Chavasse. He had a particular interest in seeing that girls were not neglected when it came time for the daily dunk, as he was convinced that the bracing effect of the ablution would strengthen the back and loins and "pave the way to becoming a mother of fine, hearty children."

The fact that writers felt the need to extol the virtues of the cold bath and offer testimonials as to its efficacy suggests that they were aware of the danger that soft-hearted mothers might flinch from their duty when confronted with a child who did not want to start her day breaking the ice as she descended into the tub. For those whose resolve was likely to be weakened in the face of their offspring's wailing and crying, the suggestion was to sing very loudly. This not only made it harder to hear the cries of protest, but also helped the baby learn that she was not, and would not be listened to; sooner or later she would accept that this daily routine was unavoidable and would benefit from the stimulation it provided to the circulatory and nervous systems.

The demise of the cold bath may have been another example of the impact of technology rather than being primarily attributable to any change in attitudes. Plumbing improved, as did methods for heating water. I suspect that more and more parents gladly opted for making bath-time an enjoyable experience, or at least one that did not evoke daily tears or rebellion. With the possible exception of headmasters of exclusive boarding schools, the advocates of the cold shower and bath no longer had a receptive audience.

Dress

Swaddling was common prior to the Victorian era; infants were tightly bandaged so that very little movement was possible. Although such a practice might seem alien or even unkind to many parents in our society, it has remained standard in other cultures. The soothing effect of being restrained is also well known to parents: while "swaddling" may no longer be recognized as a standard part of childcare, wrapping a crying baby tightly in his blanket can be a very effective means of helping him settle. The notable disadvantage of swaddling, however, was its associated lack of attention to hygiene. Babies would remain in soiled clothing for long periods of time and many suffered from chronic skin irritation as a result. The English developed the culotte to reduce this problem. This garment kept the infant secure, but had fasteners at the crotch to allow for easy access and permit attempts at toilet training.

The use of restrictive clothing persisted throughout the nineteenth century. "Binders" were used with infants, their purpose being to ensure warmth by providing a tight covering around the abdominal area. As children grew, they also tended to remain overdressed by today's standards. This eventually came to the attention of childcare writers. Along with notions of greater freedom of expression came the idea that the body should not be encumbered by endless layers of clothing, tight collars, or the heavy cloaks that were frequently part of the young child's wardrobe. Outdoor play and an emphasis on exercise required clothing to be looser and lighter.

Misconceptions regarding anatomy and physiology had a strong influence on the advice given to parents about how to dress their children. This was especially true for girls who had to endure lacing, corsets, and bodices, all designed to support the spine and abdomen. To some extent this became part of a narrow stereotype of feminine beauty: it was considered attractive to have a very narrow midriff and a tightly laced corset was

a guaranteed way to take a few inches off the waistline. But a belief in gender differences in physical qualities was also part of the justification for
what must have been a source of great discomfort for many girls. It was
argued that structural problems of the spine were more prevalent among
girls; their skeletons were weaker and they needed the added support of
rigid and tight garments. Medical thinking was to undergo an about-face,
however, and doctors eventually became vocal in their opposition to the
tight-laced undergarment. After a resurgence of this fashion towards the
latter part of the century, *The Lancet* considered the topic so critical as to
devote an article to its discussion. After a review of the damaging effects,
the writer implored girls and women to loosen up: "Once more we urge
the female members of the community to abandon this fatal article of attire. Its aesthetic function exists only in the imagination, being grounded
on the false and perverted notion that the natural contour of the body is
ungraceful, while the deformed, contracted waist is considered beautiful." This advice seems to have been unheeded by most and the use of restrictive clothing remained fashionable into the twentieth century.

Well-dressed girls of the mid-Victorian era: elegant and modest.

The assumed delicacy of girls necessitated paying particular attention
to keeping them warm. Bare legs and arms were not only immodest, they
also meant that too much of the body surface was exposed to the air. This
would disturb the circulation, disrupt blood flow to the vital areas, and dis-
astrous results were sure to follow. For Rankin, the bedroom slipper was
high on the list of childhood hazards. It was argued that a girl who forgoes
the protection of boots and woolly stockings must suffer from cold feet.
The disturbance to the bloodstream would increase the risk of pelvic disorders and place the health and life of the child in jeopardy. "One of the
first rules for young girls is to protect the feet," he argued. Just in case the

Victorian beach attire: keeping covered at all times.

mother had a closet full of slippers and seemed in good health herself, he added that, even if the wearer did not feel cold, this did not mean that chilling of the blood and associated injury to the body had not taken place. He stated that "thousands and tens of thousands die in their effort to follow the examples of those foolhardy people who defy the laws of nature." It is hard to imagine how this physician could have endured the fashion trends of the twentieth century. According to his reasoning, the advent of the miniskirt in the sixties, for example, should have eradicated almost an entire generation of young women.

The way in which children were dressed was also seen as a moral issue. Being fashionable was often discussed in a derogatory and disapproving manner, as focusing on superficial attractiveness was inconsistent with the goals of modesty and devotion to hard work. Parading little boys or girls in their finery to delight company might seem cute, but it created narcissistic children who would lose sight of the important values. A mother's entry in her 1833 diary addresses this concern: "Mary is beginning to manifest improper fondness for dress. We have had much company lately and many have spoken to her about her beautiful gown. I must dress her in such a manner that she will not attract attention."

Chavasse was a particularly outspoken critic of the fashion trends for children. Far too much was uncovered for his liking and he was especially vocal when it came to girls who exposed their upper chest or went around with bare legs. Not only were they vain and frivolous, they were on a path to destruction. "If they live to be women – which the present fashion is likely frequently to prevent – what are they? Silly, simpering, delicate, lack-a-daisical nonentities."

Boys too became slaves to fashion at times. One of the fads in their style of dress was created inadvertently by a Mrs. Frances Hodgson Burnett towards the end of the century. She wrote for children and her best-known character was Little Lord Fauntleroy. The lad started life as Cedric and was living a humble, but exemplary life in New York. He had so much going for him; "He had so sweet a temper and ways so charming that he was a pleasure to every one." As it should be, he was devoted to his mother, whom he addressed as "dearest," in keeping with the habit of his poor departed father. He was also beautiful to look at and started life with "soft, fine, gold-colored hair which went into loose rings by the time he

was six months old." As chapter one draws to a
close, Cedric is in line for being the number-
one role model for a little boy; by chapter
two he has the position clinched. It comes
to light that he is no less than the heir to a
British title, and being a lord he is adorned
accordingly. Reginald Birch's illustrations
became responsible for a deluge of Fauntleroy look-alikes whose mothers were presumably motivated by the hope that
dressing their sons in similar garb and

*Little Lord
Fauntleroy:
the ultimate
fashion statement
for boys.*

curling their hair would increase the likelihood that they too would be
sweet and charming, call them "dearest," and inherit fame and fortune.
The sales of velvet tunics and knickerbockers skyrocketed and broad-
brimmed hats and buckled shoes were a must for the stylish boy. Burnett
also created Little Saint Elizabeth for girls. Elizabeth matched Fauntleroy
for looks, personality, and charm, but in spite of the fact that she was an elegant dresser, she did not gain similar acceptance as a fashion statement.

Health and Puberty

References in childcare literature to puberty tended to focus on girls. Although puberty is a gradual process for both genders, it was often written
about as an ominous event or even a crisis for girls. The menarche, or onset of the menses, would have reinforced this notion, as it obviously constituted a significant event in female biological development that had no
parallel for boys. The predominant views regarding female anatomy and
physiology help explain why the occurrence of the menses was often
viewed with trepidation. Writers in the field stated that the uterus and
ovaries were the most vital of all female organs. It was even declared that
the uterus was the command center of the female body and that all other
structures were, in effect, built around it. This line of reasoning extended
to theories regarding the origins of disease. While the idea that disease in
one area of the body could originate from pathology in another is accurate, the view that the uterus is the most likely culprit is not. Nonetheless,
a whole array of illnesses ranging from headaches and sore throats to tuberculosis and kidney failure were frequently attributed to an underlying

disorder of the uterus. The menarche was, therefore, a sign that the uterus and ovaries were no longer dormant and that the girl needed to be watched carefully.

Parents' anxiety must also have been heightened by what we now accept as a frequent part of adolescent menstruation – that is, its irregularity. An orderly menstrual cycle would indicate that the command center was functioning reasonably smoothly; the absence of regularity, on the other hand, would suggest inadequate internal control, if not chaos.

The apprehension regarding puberty must have made it hard to see the menarche in anything but a negative light. Rankin exhorted parents to pay very careful attention to their daughters as they approached this stage. Any change in disposition was to be noted, as were fluctuations in appetite and energy levels. Signs of disturbance were to be responded to by liberal use of tonics as well as plenty of fresh air, good food, and "the society of cheerful companions." Prompt action was necessary "in order that the child may be kept as nearly as possible in a perfect state of health, and that all stumbling blocks may be removed from Nature's way in this crisis she is bringing about."

Decreased physical activity was also prescribed, partly to ensure that the girl was kept in an environment that was neither too hot nor too cold. Parties could be hazardous due to the increased room temperature. A cold foot bath during the menses was even more dangerous. Why one would be sought in the first place was uncertain, but parents were told it could lead to "a severe congestion in the pelvic region, followed frequently by inflammation and death."

As discussed in the chapter on education, mental strain was to be avoided and, in many cases, given up entirely during the menses. After all, "nature has reserved the week for the process of ovulation and each menstrual period should be passed in the recumbent position." These comments reflected the prevailing view that the reproductive organs needed to develop, and nature could only do one thing at a time; none of the body's vital nerve-force could be spared for the brain. If the reproductive system did not get its quota, there could be a high price to pay: "arrested development of the ovaries and uterus is very apt to occur, and after marriage there is a strong likelihood of a childless home."

The physicians of the era cited the moodiness that often seems to accompany puberty as evidence that all was not well with the body. The term "hysterical" is, in fact, derived from the Greek word for uterus and it was commonplace to attribute emotional outbursts or sulkiness to a malfunction of this organ. We now know that, although adolescent mood swings are more pronounced than those of adults or younger children, they are not indicative of underlying psychological instability or disturbance. For the Victorians, however, such normal moodiness would have been a danger signal; if the girl's hysterical tendencies were not promptly checked, they could eventually lead to a complete collapse of health that would persist into adulthood.

The more the Victorian parent heeded the advice offered regarding care of girls during puberty, the greater would have been the belief that the female was indeed the weaker member of the species. Girls were to be protected and their lot in life was to be "indisposed" for a sizeable portion of each month. The mythology that surrounded puberty contributed to the restrictive roles that were given to women. The girl might derive some pleasure when excused from homework or piano lessons, both of which were frowned upon during the menses, but any such bonuses would have been far outweighed by being excluded from sports, dancing, and all forms of mental stimulation. The quiet and uneventful life prescribed for the pubertal girl in the more affluent classes could extend for many years; she was to be looked after, not challenged. For boys, the absence of a uterus meant their energies could be directed upwards to the brain; the girls' physical resources, on the other hand, were to be directed to the reproductive organs. Few demands were to be placed on her and achievement beyond marriage and childbearing was not only unnecessary, but also a flagrant disobedience of a fundamental Law of Nature that would eventually be punished severely.

Doctor in the House

The incidence of infant and childhood mortality was one reason for the prominence of health-related topics in the advice given to Victorian parents. Another was the role that parents played in the care and treatment of the family. The medical profession did not have the status it enjoys today, probably because its success rate was so low when it came to prevention and treatment of disease. Diphtheria, whooping cough, measles, scarlet fever, tuberculosis, and cholera were not controlled or prevented, and even minor cuts or abrasions could lead to fatal infection. Physicians had to contend with a limited and often ineffective repertoire of treatments. Leeches were popular and could be applied to the back of the neck for headaches and to the vulvae of girls suffering from problems of the urinary tract. The poultice made from ground beetles was used for more than bedwetting and, if all else failed, an enema or dose of castor oil would at least make something happen. Leeches and the like – while somewhat unappealing – were not harmful, even if they did little to actually improve health. Other treatments, however, were more likely to kill than cure. Copious amounts of mercury, opium, and belladonna were prescribed for numerous complaints and could have fatal results.

Coupled with the relatively low success rate of prescribed treatments was the limited ability of many families to pay for a physician's services. The climate was, therefore, ideal for the proliferation of home remedies. Parents also had access to many drugs that are today subject to strict controls, even when used by medical practitioners. For much of the Victorian era, narcotics, for example, could be obtained from pharmacists by anyone with the money to cover the purchase price.

Given their responsibility for their children's health, readers of childcare literature sought information needed to treat specific disorders. Details regarding dosages were contained in a number of books. Hood stated that lettuce could be used with abandon for insomnia. Arsenic, on the other hand, had to be taken in moderation, although it was an essential item in the medicine cabinet as a cure for warts and cancers, as well as hay fever, asthma, and bronchitis. Chavasse also provided a detailed account of how to recognize common illnesses, when to call for the "medical man," and how to concoct home remedies for the less serious maladies. His recipe for the most common complaint of early infancy – gripe – was probably followed by the many thousands of mothers who acquired his book:

> Powdered Turkey Rhubarb—half a scruple
> Carbonate of Magnesia—one scruple
> Simple Syrup—three drachms
> Dill Water—eight drachms

Assuming the baby could be persuaded to swallow this brew, one to two teaspoons every four hours would cure the problem.

It was not until the 1880s that pediatrics emerged as a specialty within the medical profession. Whether through use of specific home remedies or attention to diet, clothing, or hygiene, the Victorian parent assumed far more responsibility for trying to combat disease than we would consider either reasonable or appropriate today. This role must have been extremely stressful, and the fear of failure motivated families to establish rigid practices in many areas of child-rearing.

6. Sexuality

THE VICTORIANS are often associated with large-scale denial and repression of sexuality. Such attitudes had not, however, been typical of earlier times. When the Christian gospel was carried to Britain, for example, its bearers found a people whose sexual behavior was both indiscriminate and excessive. The verdict was that "the land has been absolutely submerged under a flood of fornication." For many centuries the medical profession also recommended frequent sexual intercourse as a means of improving health, and use of prostitutes in the treatment of certain disorders might be prescribed. Parents were even advised to take steps to ensure the future sexual prowess of their sons. Fallopius (of fallopian tubes fame) urged parents to "take every pain in infancy to enlarge the privy member of boys by massage and application of stimulants since a well-grown specimen never comes amiss."

In the period leading up to the nineteenth century many physicians still held the view that excessive chastity could be harmful for men. The rationale at that time was that stored semen turned poisonous and would be reabsorbed. The Church and the medical profession did not, however, see eye to eye on this and other topics relating to sexuality. The religious campaign against sex pitted clerics against physicians. For the Church – particularly in Puritan times – fornication and homosexuality were sins against God and, as such, carried the penalty of damnation. At one time religious laws decreed sex to be illegal on Sundays, Wednesdays, and Fridays, forty days before Easter and Christmas, and three days before communion. When allowing for the additional rules that ensured frequent attendance at communion, little of the year remained for indulging one's passions. Even on those rare days when sex was permissible, it could not be enjoyed with abandon. Any departure from the missionary position was sinful and could carry a penalty of up to seven years' penance.

By the nineteenth century the differences of opinion between the Church and medical profession had, in most respects, disappeared. The Church continued to emphasize the sinful nature of sex and now physicians were adding the deterrent of sickness. It was no longer argued that abstinence could be harmful. Rather, sex was portrayed as potentially damaging through its degenerative effect on the body; the "vital fluid" had to be preserved and not wasted on such acts as masturbation or fornication. The position on the effects of reabsorption of semen was reversed; the life-giving force should be retained within the body so that it could increase the person's physical and intellectual powers. Doctor O.S. Fowler stated with authority in *Sexual Science* (1870) that "the man's excretion embodies forty times more vital-force than an equal amount of red blood right from the heart."

Elaborate arguments were put forward in support of the theory that semen had to be preserved. The noted theologian and highly successful author Sylvanus Stall took the reader on a trip through the plant and animal kingdoms to amass evidence that the act of procreation was often deadly. Although you would need a microscope to witness the event, the cells found in green pond scum apparently die after they have embraced. Cod, salmon, and shad all find reproduction to be an exhausting endeavor, a male bee is killed for his efforts, and the plumage of the male bird loses its luster after the mating season. A case study of a butterfly that had been confined to a greenhouse was even presented. Unable to satisfy its reproductive urges, its life expectancy increased from a few days to over two years. Having convinced the reader that any bells that might be heard during sex would only be ringing a death knell, he presented a case for complete abstinence unless reproduction were the object of the exercise.

The repression of sexuality resulted in extremes. The facade was exactly that – an attempt to mask the reality that the human species does not readily limit sexual expression exclusively to the minimum required for reproduction. Prostitution, for example, was big business in Victorian times. Children could be bought cheaply to work in brothels, and maidens were in particular demand, as folklore prescribed raping a virgin as a cure for venereal disease. The pornography of the time often had a sado-masochistic element; this was a far cry from the pure and chaste image that people were supposed to convey. At the other extreme was the obsession with eradicating any reminders of the base animal instincts that would set people on the path to damnation. One particularly absurd example was the practice of covering piano legs. These were traditionally curved and had previously been ignored as an example of shameless eroticism. My only comment is that, as a very amateur musician, I have had occasion to observe more than my share of piano legs and have been bitterly disappointed to date.

The advice to limit sex to its reproductive function had appeal because it answered the difficult question of how much sexual activity was safe. "The only point at which a dividing line between love and lust can be drawn is this; love seeks sexual gratification for procreation, lust seeks it for the mere pleasure of the act." The physician who made this statement was Doctor E. Miller, who was speaking at a medical conference in 1900. He was delivering a public criticism of a fellow practitioner who had been so bold as to suggest that sex within marriage did not always need to be biologically motivated. Miller stated in no uncertain terms that such opinions were the equivalent of a death sentence for those who were so foolish as to listen. Concern was expressed that other physicians would follow suit and allow the line dividing love and lust to become blurred: "If all the doctors who hear this, talk likewise to their patrons and friends, Satan himself could not employ a more successful class of agents."

The intolerance for almost all expressions of sexuality was to dominate the childcare literature. With the threat of both damnation and sickness as consequences of most aspects of sex, the message to parents was that their children were at grave risk as soon as they left the realm of total childhood innocence.

The Solitary Vice

The concern about children's sexuality can best be illustrated by reference to the views on masturbation. Doctor John Kellogg devoted a large section of his book *Plain Facts About Sexual Life* to the "solitary vice" and described it as "one of the most destructive evils ever practised by fallen man." He and other physicians in both North America and Europe were convinced of the health risks of masturbation. Lord Chesterfield in Britain expressed his abhorrence of the practice in his *Advice to His Son*. Masturbation could pervert the child and alter the course of his life forever: "By the unhappy excesses of irregular pleasures in youth, how many amiable dispositions are corrupted or destroyed?" Doctor Alexander Ross crusaded against the solitary vice in Canada in the 1890s and stated that masturbation was a "worm eating at the core of society and doing more injury than all other diseases combined." It was believed to cause consumption, urinary disease, impotence, sterility, heart disease, epilepsy, visual defects, hearing impairment, cancer of the womb, atrophy of the breasts, and clergyman's sore throat. It was also cited as a leading cause of insanity and held responsible for the presence of many of the inhabitants of lunatic asylums. As for Fallopius's view that stimulation would add to the dimensions of the privy member, case studies were presented to demonstrate that the opposite was true. According to Ross, atrophy of the penis and testes awaited the self-abuser: "The more you use the penis muscle, the weaker it becomes; but the less you use the penis muscle, the stronger it becomes." If only this law applied to other muscles, my lifestyle would allow me to realize my fantasy of being built like a Greek god.

Kellogg published from the Office of the Health Reformer in Michigan and his texts revealed a lengthy list of potential causes of sexual arousal that could provoke masturbation. Candies, cinnamon, cloves, and peppermint were considered to excite the genital organs, and a morning shot of caffeine was an invitation to moral corruption as "tea and coffee have led thousands to perdition." Added to the dietary restrictions were the limits to be placed on the child's physical activities. Lying on the abdomen was out, but there was no point rolling onto your back as this could also provoke sexual feelings. This left lying on your side, but never on a feather bed, which would have "exciting influences." Climbing was dangerous, especially if a tree were involved – the child might end up in an intimate embrace with a branch or two. Sliding down bannisters was banned for similar reasons and the evils of bicycle riding have already been discussed. You could come indoors and curl up with a good book, but the dangers were horrific: "The taste for novel-reading is like that for liquor or opium. It is never satiated. A confirmed novel-reader is almost as difficult to reform as a confirmed inebriate or opium-eater. The influence upon the mind is most damaging and pernicious." This left little more than rolling your hoop or practicing the piano, eyes cast upwards, of course.

Although the number of legitimate activities for children was quite restricted, idleness was also to be avoided; the unoccupied mind would turn its attention to forbidden and lusty thoughts. The experience of going to school was an additional source of trepidation. All it took was one corrupt student and the "evil infection spreads more rapidly than the contagium of smallpox or yellow fever, and is scarcely less fatal."

"Wicked nurses" were seen as a serious threat. There have been times when an accepted means of settling children at night was to fondle their genitals. I should add that, while such a practice today would be seen as sexual abuse, it was almost certainly not sexually motivated when used for its sedative effects in earlier centuries. Nurses charged with the day-to-day care of many children in the middle and upper classes may indeed have continued this practice and were, therefore, to be supervised closely.

The Victorian obsession with bowel movements was related to masturbation. Constipation caused localized congestion which, in turn, overstimulated the genital area. Bladder infections and hemorrhoids posed similar dangers.

In addition, it was a given that direct handling of the genitals by the child was likely to become addictive. Childcare manuals advocated that parents mount a constant watch to ensure the moral safety of their offspring. Some advised that visits to the toilet were to be supervised. It was conceded that a boy might have to handle his penis when urinating, but this was to be kept to the minimum required to ensure appropriate trajectory. This "hands-off" campaign was to be taken very seriously, as the forbidden areas of the body, once stimulated, could become irreversibly aroused. Mothers were advised "to guard their babies from all the evils that beset them. They can be taught that little children sometimes form a habit of handling themselves and as a result they become listless and sick and many times idiotic and insane, or develop epileptic fits."

The concerned parent needed to take steps to prevent undue stimulation. Recognizing that no child who was succumbing to the solitary vice would bring the topic up for discussion, advice was needed to aid in early detection. Kellogg provided a list of thirty-nine suspicious signs. These included delayed or premature physical development, bashfulness or unnatural boldness, and a fondness for, or aversion to the opposite sex. Even if a child had managed to find a safe mid-ground on these dimensions, other tendencies could betray his awakening sexuality. A distaste for play, fondness for solitude, bedwetting, poor conversational skills, inability to take a hint, forgetfulness, mock piety, lying, and lusterless eyes were all on the list. I am reminded of the precautions I took when I first lectured on the subject of Victorian attitudes towards masturbation. Round shoulders and a stooping posture were number eighteen on the list; eating chalk was number twenty-six. I made sure I stood at attention throughout the class and I never went near the blackboard.

Acne, especially on the forehead, was another potential indicator of masturbation and fingernail-biting and warts were cited as very common among girls addicted to the vice. The girl whose breast development was relatively slow was also likely to be suffering from the effects of self-pollution, and any child who shuffled or dragged his feet was a candidate for interrogation.

Kellogg acknowledged that suspicious signs were not necessarily diagnostic of the problem. There were unfortunately only a few positive, unambiguous indicators. One was catching the person in the act, and suspicious parents were advised to sneak up on the child at night and throw back the bedclothes.

All the signs were to be "thoroughly mastered by those who have children under their care." The parent had to be "on the alert to detect the signs at once when they appear, and then carefully seek for others until there is no longer any doubt about the case." Given the broad range of normal and common behaviors or complaints on the list, it would have been the rare child or adolescent who escaped suspicion or condemnation. In truth, none of the reported indicators of masturbation, with the exception of being caught in the act, would have borne any significant relationship to sexual feelings and practices.

But what of the fallen child who had become a slave to his sexual impulses? Was there any cure? Some thought not. The founder of a major teaching hospital in London, Doctor Maudsley, summed up his view of the matter as follows: "I have no faith in the employment of physical means to check what has become a serious mental disease; the sooner he sinks to his degraded rest the greater for himself and the better for the world which is well rid of him." Others, although not particularly optimistic, held out at least a measure of hope that the child's moral, spiritual, and physical health could be improved, if not restored completely. The suspected masturbator, or even the child who simply showed an interest in her sexual organs, should first be severely reprimanded and, if old enough, treated to a lengthy lecture regarding her impending doom. Quoting Fowler's treatise in *Sexual Science* would have fit the bill: "If you cannot conquer now you never can. Make one desperate struggle. Touch not, taste not, handle not, lest you perish with the using. Flee at once to perfect continence, your only city of refuge. Will you long debate which of the two to choose, slavery and death, and such a death, or abstinence and life?"

Duly cautioned, the child was not to be left unattended and had to be fully occupied by work, study, or wholesome recreation. Daily exercise would relieve local congestion in the genitalia and was to be carried on to the point of fatigue so that the child would want to do no more than sleep when he went to bed. But even when asleep, the child was at risk. Although less threatening than masturbation, nocturnal emissions, or "wet

Sinking to his degraded rest: the eventual fate of the child who masturbated.

dreams," could drain the vital force. The belief that it was necessary to sleep on the side rather than back or abdomen led to methods for preventing shifts of position during the night. Tying a towel around the child's abdomen with the knot over the lower back was one method; another was to tie one hand to the bedpost. Kellogg cautioned that feather pillows and beds would produce heat in the private parts; a hair mattress or a bed of corn husks or wood shavings, on the other hand, made "a very healthful and comfortable bed."

Dreams were to be controlled or eliminated. "Nocturnal pollutions" were almost always connected with "dreams of a lascivious nature." All that was necessary was that the child or adolescent have the determination to combat unchaste thoughts. With sufficient resolve, this should be possible at night, just as it was during the day.

After spending a dreamless night trussed up on a bed of corn husks, the child could look forward to a hearty breakfast. "Hearty" did not, however, mean pancakes or eggs and bacon. After eliminating the foods and spices that were supposed to excite the passions, little was left aside from fruits, grains, and vegetables. Two names stand out in the search for a healthy, mind-improving diet. The first is Reverend Graham who was a strong proponent of unprocessed foods. He became a cult figure in early Victorian times and his followers were known as Grahamites. His chief legacy was the Graham cracker. The second figure of note was Doctor Kellogg himself, who apparently owed his unblemished character partly to his habit of starting each day with seven Graham crackers. He also developed his own health foods; the most famous of which is corn flakes. The irony is that the company that still bears his name now markets breakfast cereals that contain many of the items that were on his list of forbidden substances, such as sugar and cinnamon. For Kellogg, the distribution of Cruncheroos would have been every bit as dangerous as the invasion of ballet dancers.

If such measures were felt to be insufficient, the intervention took an increasingly aggressive, if not brutal quality. It was not uncommon for small children to be put to bed with their hands tied together; specially sized handcuffs were also marketed. Another technique was placing a child in a garment much like the straitjacket that was used to restrict vio-

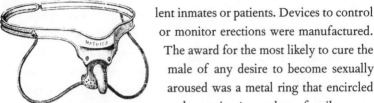

Weapons used in the "hands-off" campaign.

lent inmates or patients. Devices to control or monitor erections were manufactured. The award for the most likely to cure the male of any desire to become sexually aroused was a metal ring that encircled the penis. A number of spikes protruded from its inner edge, ready to impale the penis should an erection occur. Alternatively, a gauge could be placed around the penis that triggered an alarm if sufficiently stretched. Sleep studies over the past few decades have established that all healthy males, from birth to senescence, spend approximately one-third of sleep with a partial or full erection. These erections seem to have nothing to do with sexual arousal, but reflect normal physiological changes that occur during certain stages of sleep. The parents who were awakened by the sounds of bells or yells of pain would have been convinced, however, that they had a disturbed, depraved child on their hands.

The Society for Orificial Surgeons had strong views regarding the prevention and treatment of childhood sexuality. Its members believed firmly in the dangers of the foreskin or prepuce. This could stimulate the penis, either through movement over the tip or because of infection that developed due to inadequate hygiene. The influence of this society contributed to the widespread use of circumcision in North America. "The Prepuce as an Outlaw" was one of the many articles published by the society's members in which the urgency of circumcision for boys was declared. Numerous case studies were presented to support the claims of miraculous cures that had followed this surgical procedure.

Attention was subsequently turned to the question of female masturbation. According to Stall, a girl's worst thought should be "whiter than her pretty hand." Anything but complete disinterest in sexuality was unacceptable. To hold hands with a boy was to ruin one's reputation and, once lost, it could never be recovered. Physicians were, therefore, reluctant to even acknowledge that a girl could indulge in any practice which violated the ideal of feminine purity. Kellogg pronounced that "we have the greatest difficulty in making ourselves believe that it is possible for beings, designed by nature to be pure and innocent, in all respects free from impurity of any sort, to become so depraved by sin as to be willing to devote themselves to so vile and filthy a practice." The fact that increasing numbers seemed to be falling from grace could not, however, be ignored and steps were needed to deal with the problem. "The girls have been neglected," wrote Kellogg. "I do feel an irresistible impulse to cry out against the shameful neglect of the clitoris and its hood because of the vast amount of sickness and suffering which could be saved for the gentler sex if this important subject received proper attention. Circumcision for the girl is as necessary as for the boy." Surgical removal of the clitoris was, therefore, advised for the girl given to, or suspected of the solitary vice, although less drastic techniques might first be tried, such as stitching the labia together to render the clitoral region inaccessible. In addition to being cruel and unnecessary, these procedures exposed young people to the high risk of infection that accompanied any form of surgery.

Birds and Bees

Very little information seems to have been given to parents on the topic of sex education. Sexuality remained a taboo subject. While parents had to be on guard for its unwelcomed arrival, they should not broach the subject ⟍ unnecessarily. The myth of the sexless child was to be challenged by Freud, but until then the notion that childhood should be devoid of any sexual impulses was subscribed to and promoted. With this attitude firmly in their minds, many writers seemed to adopt the view that any type of sex education for children was unnecessary.

As evident from their preoccupation with masturbation, however, the Victorians were aware that innocence could be lost prematurely. This gave rise to a debate as to whether or not it would be advisable to provide some form of instruction to keep any aberrant impulses firmly in check. Doctor Miller published his thoughts on the matter in the *Journal of Orificial Surgery* (1894). He had no doubt that such instruction was not only warranted, but could also be the key to salvation. Referring to the large number of children who had inherited strong sexual passions from their misguided parents, he argued that, without proper education, most would become "physical, moral, and mental wrecks." Writing in the same period, another physician, on the other side of the Atlantic, Doctor Acton, also advocated early intervention, although boys were his specific target: "The essence of all this training of the will, however, lies in beginning early. If a boy is once fully impressed that all such indulgences are dirty and mean, and with the whole force of his unimpaired energy determines he will not disgrace himself by yielding, a very bright and happy future is before him."

This type of instruction gradually became included in the curricula for older students. "Purity agents" visited schools, but their role was clearly to warn adolescents of the perils associated with lust rather than helping them develop a greater understanding of sexuality. The term "sex education" was not even employed at this time; this would have been too blatant and the euphemism "social hygiene" was coined instead.

The deliberate introduction of discussion regarding sex did not, however, meet with universal approval. Some portrayed it as an ill-advised practice that might put ideas into young minds. "To inflame the tender mind of a young boy or girl with such information is criminal," was Doctor Mean's opinion in his presentation to his fellow orificial surgeons in 1893. The ensuing debate became furious at times: Mean's opinion that early instruction would "eternally and irreparably ruin a boy or girl" was countered by a fellow physician who maintained that there would be "thousands of boys and girls irreparably ruined for want of such advice." The proponents of at least some form of sex education also made the point that, if parents and others responsible for children's upbringing did not provide information, somebody else almost surely would. The risk according to Miller was that, instead of receiving accurate advice, they would fall prey to an evil-minded companion who would "poison their minds with lustful teachings."

It was recognized that children might also ask questions – the most common concerning how babies come into the world. Fables and fairy tales were not recommended by most writers, but the truth was hardly suitable for tender ears. Creative approaches were developed. The parent might, for example, use a complex, technical, and flowery vocabulary that would be indecipherable to all but English majors. After one or two lines of this hyperbole the child would remain as uninformed as before, but would lose all interest in pursuing the matter. For those with more meager vocabularies, there were always the tales of union between fish, birds, and bees to save the day. No doubt there were children who were also treated to accounts of how green scum gets to cover a whole pond. These lessons from nature, however, were supposed to be cursory and obscure, leaving few, if any, clues as to the details of human sexual behavior.

The tendency to provide sex education that includes anything but the information of importance or interest to young people has been enduring. I recall leaving school with far more understanding of how flowers reproduced than I had of procreation in my own species. My best friend and "evil-minded companion" had offered his opinion on the matter, but his information was suspect. I hope to locate him on my next visit to England as I want to know if he has a family; from what he told me, this would be a biological impossibility. For the Victorian child, however, ignorance must have been accompanied by a level of fear and anxiety that would have remained high into adulthood.

7. Mother Knows Best?

OVER THE PAST few decades it has become commonplace for both parents to be employed outside the home. The efforts made by women to obtain parity in the work force have resulted in an acknowledgment that they are not only able to compete in the field of employment, but can also continue to be effective as parents. It has also created a new image for women: the Supermom. The image highlights an injustice inherent in many families today: while attempts have been made to increase men's involvement in childcare, women still perform most of the duties in the home. This is aptly illustrated by the picture of the working mother preparing supper and attending to the children, while the no-longer-working father retires to the armchair with his newspaper.

The move to involve fathers more in family life follows a lengthy period of gender role stereotyping that went largely unchallenged. But the strict division of duties and responsibilities between husbands and wives has not always existed. It is also not characteristic of most cultures today; anthropological studies have indicated that it is only the minority of societies in which the mother assumes primary or exclusive responsibility for young children.

One of the reasons for the development of distinct roles for mothers and fathers in Western civilization was the change that occurred in the economic basis of the family. Prior to Victorian times all members of the family often remained together throughout much of the day. Home industries were common and the routine of the father leaving the home in the morning to go to work was by no means standard. When advice was offered regarding child-rearing it was, therefore, directed towards both parents. With the development of commerce and industry during the nineteenth century, however, employment outside the home became more frequent. The "work" of the family became divided into two components: domestic duties and paid outside employment. The former was designated as women's work and, together with the dwindling number of extended, multigenerational households, this came to mean "mothers' work." The latter was the province of the man.

This division of labor was to become an assumed aspect of society in Victorian times. Men were to be freed to run the world, while women renewed its population. The problem that arose for a number of men, however, was that, while they did not particularly want to become involved in childcare themselves, they were not too sure that women could be trusted to do a good job. The childcare literature of the nineteenth century, therefore, placed emphasis on the role of the mother, but did not necessarily portray her in a positive light. Again, the era was one of extremes, with opposing positions each finding powerful advocates from many quarters.

The Mother as Queen

By early Victorian times a mother could expect to be the primary caregiver. Schools were yet to become a standard part of children's lives, so she would often have their company every day of the week. The gradual decline in infant mortality over the century also meant she could anticipate raising more of her offspring until they reached adulthood; mothering had become a long-term and full-time career.

The job description for mothers was straightforward: raise a generation of God-fearing and hard-working citizens. This task assumed great importance in the minds of both men and women, and society at large had an increasing interest in how children were being reared. There was a growing need for skilled and industrious people in the work force. Business and commerce required managers and leaders, and the professions were expanding. The mothers of the educated classes were, therefore, charged with the critical responsibility of providing the young adults who would ensure that the nation remained competitive. Moreover, some feared that the lower classes or certain racial groups that were deemed inferior would gradually take over by sheer force of numbers if the upper echelons of society did not maintain their edge through careful breeding and superior child-rearing. John Abbott was one of those who voiced concern about the state of the world and there was no doubt in his mind regarding who should take on the task of correcting matters. It would be the mothers who would "bring back our guilty race to duty and happiness," he wrote in *The Mother at Home*. Society and its most critical institution – the family – were in peril, and mothers would be the "chief instruments in its redemption." The relationship between the mother and the quality of existence was plain: "When our land is filled with virtuous and patriotic mothers, then it will be filled with virtuous and patriotic men."

Abbott was an unswerving supporter of the view that the mother was almost the sole determinant of the child's personality and behavior. "His character is in your hands, and you are to form it for good or for evil," was a statement that he repeated in many forms throughout his discussion of the mother's role in family life. As did other writers, he held up Washington and Byron as the prime examples of how the mother's influence could mold a saint or create a sinner. George's mother was much revered for raising the child who was so honest and courageous that he not only confessed to chopping down a cherry tree, but also went on to become the founding president of the United States. Byron, on the other hand, may have penned some pretty impressive lines in his time, but he was nonetheless a career reprobate. Abbott expressed no doubt regarding their differing fates: "Had Byron and Washington exchanged cradles during their infancy, Washington might have been the licentious profligate and Byron the exemplar of virtue." To reinforce his position, he reminded the reader of the alarming number of "lunatics, dissolutes, and vile adults" who were the direct result of poor mothering.

The regal status of motherhood was also a theme in women's writings during this period. Author A. J. Graves was an advocate of greater respect for her gender. In many respects she saw the mother and father as occupying positions of comparable status and she asserted that, "as a rational and moral being she is man's equal." She did not, however, want women to venture beyond their traditional roles and her castigation of the "fashionable woman" was unflinching. Speaking out against women who neglected their "true and allotted sphere – domestic life," she quoted statistics from the 1839 Secretary of the Treasury report. In comparison to the paltry $352,446 that had been spent on importing items relating to science and the arts, a whopping $20,474,454 went to the silk trade so that the indolent women of the day could devote their attention and family income to "gaudy articles of dress." This loss of traditional values horrified Mrs. Graves and she deplored its effects on the next generation: "Before the child can speak, its attention is directed to the pretty frock, the gay riband, and the golden-clasped necklace. This graves upon the infant heart the indelible lesson that personal decorations and mere external beauty are more to be desired than anything else." Her antidote to the ills of society was for women to recognize that they had a primary and God-given obligation to devote their lives to the care and guidance of their children. While not opposed to education for girls, she had strong opinions on the content of the curriculum. The object was not to equip young ladies for outside pursuits such as employment or politics, but to prepare them to tend to the many physical, moral, and spiritual needs of their family.

Although the mother's responsibility was awesome, she was promised endless joy and satisfaction. She had, of course, the assurance that ten thousand raptures were about to thrill her bosom. If the mother who was confronted with a large family progeny, but none of the advantages of indoor plumbing and morning cartoons, was beginning to tire of waiting for the first rapture, she could at least expect ample reward in the afterlife. Lydia Child, who seemed to make no distinction between motherhood and paradise, commented: "Does not the little cherub in his way guide you to heaven, marking the pathway by the flowers as he goes?" Speaking frankly, "no" would have been my guess, but perhaps too many years of child-rearing have left me jaded. In similar vein, I wonder if my wife and I have set our sights far too low when it comes to our expectations regarding the rewards that will be ours once the children are grown up and able to repay us for our years of selfless devotion to their care. I suspect Kathy would happily settle for the occasional invitation at Christmas, a collect call on Mother's Day, and the experience of watching them voluntarily hang up their coats when they visit. This pales in comparison to the dividends promised by Abbott. He predicted with confidence that properly managed children would grow up to "revere you and be the solace of your declining years." In tribute, they would use their mother as the model for raising their own offspring and, like a chain letter, there would be an exponential return on her investment. In this idyllic picture of the autumn of life, Abbott envisaged a serene matriarch whose children and grandchildren had elevated her to saintlike status and lived for little reason other than showering her with love and veneration: "And when your children's children cluster around you, giving unceasing tokens of respect and affection, you will find in their caresses the renewal of your youth." Moving on to her reserved spot in paradise, mother would prepare the eternal abode for those who would some day follow. Although her departure would be mourned, she could leave content in the knowledge that she had trained her children to be "heirs of a glorious immortality."

.The realities of life in the nineteenth century placed heavy demands on mothers – particularly those who did not have the financial resources to employ servants. Complaints were not, however, to be voiced or even expected; given her exalted role and her promised riches, her gratitude was supposed to increase with each new load of laundry and sink full of dishes. After all, Sylvanus Stall had observed that "an idle woman is always an unhappy woman. Her household duties are no misfortune, but a blessing." The fact that he had presumably never been blessed himself did not seem to deter him from adding that domestic activities would awaken "that which is noblest and best in a woman's nature" and bring her happiness, health, and long life. Chavasse added allure to this list, pronouncing that the mother "never looks so charming as when she is attending to her household duties."

But it was not only men who proposed this model of family life. One sign of the elevated status of motherhood was that women began to be accepted as authorities on children and many put pen to paper to extol the virtues of hearth and home. What was to cause frustration and sometimes outrage among the few active feminists, however, was that, while motherhood was obviously a legitimate and worthy pursuit, no other option was permissible. The woman was not to proceed beyond the confines of the home. She could not aspire to being the next president or prime minister, but was to be content with the prospect of perhaps raising one. Books often reminded her that numerous famous people had expressed heartfelt and immeasurable gratitude to their mothers, and the truism that behind every successful man was a mother was supposed to compensate for the lack of opportunity to achieve in the work force herself.

I find it strange that a number of writers presented none other than Queen Victoria as the role model par excellence. It was pointed out that, royal though she might be, she did not shy away from her responsibility as a mother of nine children. The contradiction in my mind, however, is that while the run-of-the-mill mother was supposed to be content with her domestic duties, Queen Victoria held a full-time job and, in the realms of power and financial status, had done rather well for herself.

Placing mothers at the center of family life did not, however, guarantee tribute. As long as a child was deemed a success story, the mother was to be given full credit, and childcare writers could be more than generous in their use of superlatives when composing the accolades bestowed upon the woman who had fulfilled her obligation to family and society. But if her little cherub ended up scattering thistles instead of flowers upon the pathways of life, she was fully to blame; she had the destiny of the world in her hands and she had better not fail. If she did, Abbott, in writing in *The Mother at Home,* condemned her to eternal guilt. Even if the mother had somehow managed to slip into heaven, her children would drop by to haunt her on their way to the place set aside for those who have spent their time on earth as dissolutes and otherwise vile adults. He described the scene in detail: "When you meet your children at the bar of God, and they point to you and say, 'It was your neglect of duty which banished us from Heaven and consigned us to endless woe,' you must feel what no tongue can tell. Oh, it is dreadful for a mother to trifle with duty. Eternal destinies are committed to your trust."

Restricting a woman to marriage and motherhood had, of course, left no other way of evaluating her achievements; the success of her children was the single means by which she could demonstrate her worth. Many middle- and upper-class families employed servants, but it was the mother who was responsible for the children's upbringing. Manuals often made reference to the heinous influences of ignorant and evil servants and advised mothers to monitor their activities very carefully. It was acceptable to involve servants in childcare, but scrupulous supervision had to be in place. Whatever arrangements were made, the blame for any problems that arose fell on the mother's shoulders as the person in charge.

It would also have been to no avail for the mother to blame any perceived failures on factors beyond her control, such as heredity. It was no longer believed that human nature was predetermined almost exclusively according to divine will. Rather, children were seen as malleable and, in keeping with the popular metaphors, the mother was the sculptor who would shape the clay, or the gardener who would cultivate her little rosebuds. Only she had the unique and special qualities needed; the important instincts, abilities, and attachments were *maternal,* not *parental* and she was accountable for the quality of the finished product.

Similarly, it would have been difficult for a mother to alleviate her feelings of guilt and blame by pointing out that the child had become subject to many sources of influence outside the home. While Victorian mothers often expressed trepidation regarding the effects of the child's association with others in the community and at school, they were even more vocal in their belief that the foundation of personality and behavior was laid in the very early years. Abbott added his opinion that a negative impact of the educational system had been to create the expectation that schools could provide the type of guidance and early training that were, in fact, the mother's prescribed duty to provide. He made it clear that it was impossible for the school, however fine an institution it might be, to "purify the streams which are flowing from a corrupt fountain."

The mother's status as a parent, together with the emphasis on the role of early experiences, rendered her the prime target when children did not meet the expectations society had for correct and constructive behavior. If a scapegoat were needed, the mother was the obvious candidate; almost anything could be, and was, attributed to the baby's early experiences and it was the mother who had been responsible for upbringing during this period.

Mothers Dethroned

By the mid-Victorian period, the pressure was on to upgrade society and mothering became serious business. More and more was written by way of advice regarding how to raise healthy children, and journals and magazines were devoted to the topic, just as they are today. Initially an author could be considered qualified simply by virtue of being of generally sound and respectable character. A theology or medical degree never hurt, but a woman without academic qualifications could find a willing publisher. As long as it was believed that instincts and other innate qualities peculiar to a woman were the key to successful child-rearing, her gender afforded her status.

It seems to be a foible of human nature that the more power and status given to people, the more others will be tempted to mount a takeover bid. A growing and persistent chorus of voices challenging women's competence as parents was to be heard during the latter part of the Victorian era. Men never lost their willingness to allow women to darn their socks, change diapers, and cook the meals, but many became less confident that mothers should have such a dominant role in shaping the world's future through child-rearing. A new set of beliefs regarding how a person became a good parent was developed that reflected the rise of scientific thinking during this period of history. Attributes that had once been described as strengths were now redefined as liabilities. The mother's attachment to her child could detract from her objectivity – it made her far too emotional and sentimental. The concept of maternal instinct also lost its stature; the job was too complicated just to be left to innate feelings or tendencies. Instead of trusting nature, education and training were necessary for the mother, and the stage was set for the arrival of the professional expert. This new breed of adviser came almost exclusively from the professions and, although there were notable exceptions, most were men. To speak with authority the person needed to be highly educated; doctors and theologians were to be listened to by virtue of their training and it was of no interest or relevance if they had no experience in the day-to-day care of children. Their role was primarily to supervise; the experts now sat in the throne and mothers were supposed to be their subjects.

The advent of the new class of experts and the emphasis on scientific approaches to child-rearing have not been portrayed in historical texts as exerting an exclusively negative influence on the status of motherhood. As seems characteristic of so many developments, the reviews have been mixed. The trend towards scientific thinking meant that efforts were made to gather knowledge and data so that approaches to child-rearing could be improved. How truly "scientific" these efforts were is open to much debate, but at least childcare was being seen as a legitimate topic for serious study. Child psychology became an established pursuit at universities, and research was conducted that addressed issues concerning development and parenting. Interest groups and associations spread. Hall's Child Study Movement brought mothers and professionals together for the purpose of disseminating information, gathering data, and discussion of topics relevant to most parents. While the attitude that advice and knowledge was to flow primarily from the expert down to the audience of mothers can justifiably be criticized as presumptuous and, in some respects, demeaning, the movement did establish childcare as a field that deserved serious attention.

The declining acceptance of the woman as the innate possessor of all the qualities needed to be a mother was by no means an orderly, even trend. The emphasis on childcare as a science that should be directed by the professional expert was not always evident in the literature. The same authors that made numerous references to the need to consult professionals and obey the laws they had discovered would also wax lyrical about the mother's inherent virtues. The cynical side of my nature, however, makes me suspect that such flattery might have been motivated by a need to counteract the consequences of overdoing the criticisms that had been leveled at them. The writers may have been concerned that too many attacks on mothers' integrity could lead to mass resignations and suggestions that perhaps the experts should show them how it was to be done. It also appears that anxiety regarding women seeking work outside the home led to deliberate efforts to convince mothers that they were valued and special. The educated classes apparently followed birth-rate statistics as closely as stock market prices and each new dip renewed the fears concerning the growth of the undesirable strata of society. In North America, the most obvious example of an attempt to ensure that mothers knew their importance (and therefore their place) occurred a short while after Victoria's death – namely, the creation of Mother's Day.

Has Anyone Seen Dad?

When they were not busy running the world or cloistered in their offices writing books about family life, what were the fathers doing? Society in the nineteenth century was patriarchal; both social convention and the laws on the statute books established that men had far greater power than women. Even during the period when the mother was the undisputed expert in the field of childcare, the father retained the veto. It was assumed that he should be the ultimate authority in the home and this arrangement was presented as best for everyone. "Why should it be so terrible to acknowledge that your husband is nobler and larger than yourself?" asked Reverend Goss in *Husband, Wife and Home*. "Be thankful it is so. Try to climb up on his broad shoulders and see the world through his eyes. What an opportunity to be in such close contact with an intelligence and character so much greater than your own." Having thrown all modesty to the wind, he offered this advice: "Bend your proud little neck to the yoke of his judgement. Sit at his feet and learn. Sometimes his mind has so much wider sweep than yours that it will be far better for you to be like a child than a wife." He did acknowledge that it was possible for there to be situations in which the wife and mother knew more and should be listened to with respect. The question of who was superior was not in dispute, however; a subordinate can have good ideas, but a subordinate she remains.

I am intrigued by the ingenuity employed by male authors in their efforts to maintain the status quo. Rather than use the assumption of innate feeble-mindedness to keep women in their place, Professor Wayland tried the novel argument that subservience was nothing but good fortune in disguise. "The act of submission," he claimed in *The Elements of Moral Science*, "is in every respect as dignified and as lovely as the act of authority."

On top of this equality, women were, in truth, bestowed with greater honor than the male of the species through their power to influence young minds. Not surprisingly, he never hints that the genders should trade positions so that men could have a turn at receiving such honor. A variation on the "see how lucky you really are" theme came from William Alcott. Woman was created to be angelic and in her elevated capacity she "rules the world." The punch line was to come: "The greatest of rulers, after all, is he or she who serves most." Of course, women were afforded the privilege of serving the most so that they could be exalted.

The superiority of man also met without challenge from Mrs. Graves. She held that the genders had started out on an even playing field. The problem, once again, was the Fall. Adam and Eve disobeyed God and "woman was made subject to man, both as a punishment for her share in the transgression and as a condition best suited to their lapsed state." She reasoned that someone had to take the helm to steer mankind back to a state of grace. Although it must have seemed obvious to Mrs. Graves that Adam would get the captain's job, she never explains her reasoning or makes mention of the male share of the punishment.

In principle, therefore, the father as head of the household had a great deal of potential to influence the upbringing of the children. How much he actually utilized this potential is an entirely different matter. More and more men worked away from home. Their hours of employment were long by today's standards and were often spread over six days. As a result, it would have been very difficult for most men to take a very active role in childcare. Writers also appear to have assumed that whatever time was spent in the home would be devoted to pursuits that had nothing to do with children. One manual for husbands set aside four chapters to espouse the merits of letter-writing, keeping a journal, novel-reading, and the employment of tasteful jokes and puns, but left no space for a discussion of fatherhood.

The decline of highly authoritarian and punitive methods of raising children also had an effect on the father's position. The expression "wait till your father comes home" has probably been associated too strongly with Victorian times. It denotes a type of family in which the sins of the day were accumulated, with punishment in the form of a beating being postponed until the father returns and is handed the rod on his way through the door. Although such approaches to discipline would have been found in some families, the trend was towards gentler forms of control that required dealing with problems as they arose as opposed to handing down a sentence that would be carried out later by the "enforcer."

When the fathers' involvement was suggested in the advice manuals it was usually for one of two purposes. The first was to make sure they did not forget their overall responsibility for keeping everyone else in the family in line. The second was to take particular care that their children's spiritual needs were being met. This was an obvious area in which the father could be more involved: while it would not have been unusual for children to see very little of him from Monday to Saturday, he could be expected to put in an appearance on the Sabbath. Alcott saw no end to the potential return on this weekly investment of time. If Jesus had managed to found Christianity by focusing His efforts on a mere twelve disciples, the combined efforts of god-fearing men on their wives and children could surely stem the tides of evil. Exhorting a father to "first exert a holy and heavenly influence on his wife and family" Alcott asked, "Is there anything more plain than if every individual would feel the responsibility of doing what I have alluded to, the world would, in a short time, become what it ought to be?" He applied math to support his contention that each and every father could have a tremendous influence on society. Based on the assumption that each father had five children, he calculated that each reader could spawn 19,530 more Christians by the year 2000. Projecting even further, he concluded that the "eternal well-being of hundreds of millions may depend on the efforts of a single husband."

In spite of the factors that supported fathers' maintaining a peripheral position in the family, there was the occasional voice urging them to see the merits and benefits of parenthood. Stall gave center stage to mothers in the home, but saw an important role for fathers as well: "Some husbands speak of 'the baby' as if it belonged wholly to his wife, not to them. The thought of caring for or tending the child seems to be foreign to their minds." In his criticism of such views he decreed that "it is not only the father's duty, but it ought also to be his pleasure to look after his own children." He added that the experience of holding and caring for one's child was an honor, as well as a source of satisfaction. He argued that fathers were to see the baby as a blessing and that the "little woman" could not, and should not, do it all. Anticipating some resistance to his ideas, he addressed the inhibitions that fathers needed to overcome, reassuring them that they could still be real men even if spied by friends and neighbors wheeling the baby carriage in the park. Advice of this nature was, however, neither frequent nor prominent in childcare literature and it seems unlikely that it had a profound impact on the thinking of the period.

8. Facts, Fantasies, and Theories

E XPERTS DO NOT typically offer advice in a random or haphazard
manner; each has a particular set of beliefs regarding how children
develop and what determines their personality and behavior.
These theories may be fashionable for a time, only to be replaced by another set of assumptions. To take an example from education, there were
Victorians who subscribed to the theory that too much brain-work would
deplete the supply of vital energy in the body and impede the child's physical development. Today such a theory seems absurd – one of its predic-
tions would be that a junior gifted class would be populated by feeble
midgets. An alternative theory from the nineteenth century was that early
stimulation, provided it was not accompanied by excessive pressure, was a
very positive and important part of children's development. A large seg-
ment of the toy industry catered to those who held this belief and educational television for preschoolers today would not be commercially viable
if this particular theory had not prevailed.

The Victorian era illustrates how powerful theories can be in deter-
mining views about all aspects of child-rearing. It also illustrates how easy

it is to forget the distinction between fact and theory; too often what has been presented as a body of knowledge has proved to be no more than speculation and fantasy.

The Laws of Human Nature

For centuries religion had provided the explanation of why things happened the way they did. God had made the world and only He understood its many mysteries. He preordained certain people to be saints, while others were born to be career sinners. Some died young – often for no obvious reason – but it was assumed to be God's will.

The Church continued to be very strong throughout the nineteenth century. What changed, however, was the status of religion as an explanatory system. God remained omnipotent, but science emerged as an additional, and sometimes very powerful means of understanding the world. Tremendous advances were made in biology, anatomy, physiology, and medicine. The more childhood diseases could be prevented by vaccination and improved hygiene, the more people became aware that they could exert control over events. A person's life expectancy, and the quality of that life, were subject to direct intervention by humans rather than being a matter determined solely by divine forces. The understanding of the internal workings of the body grew, and with it came the idea of lawful cause-and-effect relationships. References to nature's laws were common. These were seen as governing the delicate balance between the many different systems within the body; what happened in one system did not have only a local effect, but could influence the whole organism and would do so in a predictable way. Diet provides an illustration of this principle. The advances made in nutrition have been cited as one of the most important factors in improving the general health of the population in the nineteenth century. These advances occurred in the context of increased scientific knowledge regarding how food substances influenced growth and reduced risk of illness and disease. The society that ate properly would be stronger, smarter, and more successful. At times the "laws" regarding the relationship between diet and human functioning proved to be inaccurate; the underlying principle remained, however – namely, that science had the potential to allow people to understand and possibly change what happened.

The scientific perspective gave a great deal of power to those who were involved in raising children. It was not a question of caring for the infant and watching her grow as the divine plan unfolded. Children's development could be understood in terms of more tangible and accessible factors, some of which could be controlled.

Facts, Fantasies, and the Scientific Method

The psychology departments I attended as a student were obsessive when it came to the scientific method. An innocent "good morning" could be met with a demand for proof, and any self-esteem you had before presenting a seminar would be crushed as your so-called friends and fellow students found or created as many holes as possible in your reasoning and conclusions. Our professors told us that the universe might be lawful, but reminded us time and time again that proof for any proposed law was both essential and hard to obtain. Our animal psychology professor, for example, assured us that the movement of the lowly maggot was governed by light-orienting reflexes. None of us cared deeply about this matter and we would have been more than prepared just to take his word for this aspect of invertebrate behavior. But we offered no objection when presented with a jar full of maggots at the start of the two-hour lab in which we were to gather the data needed to validate his statement.

We were taught that the rules of the scientific method were straightforward: create as many theories as you like, but make sure they lead to hypotheses that can be tested. If the data support a particular hypothesis, and your findings have more relevance to the general population than the meanderings of maggots, share your discovery with the rest of the world.

Unfortunately, the Victorians had a weakness for skipping an essential part of the scientific process. They loved to publish their conclusions, but must have found the business of generating hypotheses and gathering data to be tiresome. Much of what was written about childcare was of the "because I said so" variety and authors must have believed that they had unique access to truth. Chavasse exemplified this faith in the validity of his opinions when he commented, "I only tell what I know." Like numerous others, however, he took ideas that must have begun as pure speculation and presented them as either facts or nature's laws, without considering the need for objective, corroborative evidence. For example, to be able to examine the relationship between hours of schooling and disorders in adolescence would require a sophisticated research design and a lot of time and money. The fact that such research was absent did not deter writers from stating with authority that such a relationship existed. Similarly, the lack of research did not stop experts outlawing bicycle saddles, nursery rhymes, bedroom slippers, and homework, and decreeing that playing marbles or sprinkling cinnamon on your French toast were bound to inflame the passions. Occasionally reference might be made to the author's personal observations or to the reported observations of others. Although such data can be highly subjective and biased, writers acted as if they had a hot line to the truth and should be afforded the status of the scientist without meeting the basic requirements for scientific enquiry and conclusions.

Phrenology: The Science of Bumps

One prime example of the pseudoscientist was the phrenologist. If you take the time to feel the surface of the top portion of your head you will notice it is not as smooth as you might have assumed. Moving your fingers slowly, you will discover ridges, dips, and small protrusions. Having reached a new depth of understanding of your anatomy you will want to know its significance. Here's where the phrenologist will help you. Although there were different schools of thought, phrenologists such as Professor L.N. Fowler typically divided the head into approximately forty areas, and charts were published mapping out their location. Each area had its own function. Are you one of those people who gets homesick and just cannot seem to get ahead in life? Check the back of your head and you should find a bump roughly in the middle. If this is large, you have discovered the reason: you have a highly developed "inhabitiveness" faculty. "Your love of home and country is very strong indeed and you are liable to the most terrible feelings of homesickness when absent from them. You prefer poverty and humblest position in life at home to wealth and station abroad. To you, be it ever so humble, there is no place like home!"

Discussing one's lumps publicly is perhaps unseemly, but the elevation in the area in front of my ears is quite something to behold. My large

"alimentiveness" center dictates that I should never submit myself again
to the tortures of a diet. I have an overpowering appetite and must accept
that I "live to eat rather than eat to live."

At the core of the theory was the premise that human nature consisted
of a number of inherited temperaments, each of which was related to the
activity of a localized area of the brain. The claim of phrenology was that
it had discovered the location and function of all the important areas.
Studying the contours of the head, therefore, permitted a detailed analy-
sis of the individual's personality.

Phrenologists were taken very seriously by many Victorians, and in-
stitutes and journals devoted to the field were established in Europe and
North America. In 1850, Queen Victoria herself summoned the noted
phrenologist Doctor Combe to see the Prince of Wales. Barely eight years
old, the prince was already driving his royal parents and tutor to the brink
of despair and it was hoped that his unruly behavior could be curtailed if
he had his head examined.

At its peak, phrenology was presented as the complete science of human behavior. For only ten cents you could buy a booklet that would explain how to use phrenology to select a mate; "may I hold your hand?"
was presumably replaced by "may I feel your bumps?" Prospective maternal qualities could also be ascertained by a quick study of the back of
the head. This location was the seat of the "philoprogenitiveness" center
containing all the instincts and traits relating to motherhood. According
to Fowler, a well-developed area meant that "your love for children and
pets is intense" and was to the point where you would become an overly
indulgent, pampering parent. At the other extreme, you were destined to
be "cold and indifferent towards your children, and to manifest a positive
dislike for all others." Presumably you would also be quick to flush ailing
goldfish without so much as a pang of conscience. Queen Victoria, of
course, had a healthy, but not excessive protrusion in this area, as was illustrated by the profile of her contained in one manual.

Phrenology was used to explain the vagaries of childhood development. Manuals were published that advised both parents and teachers to
use this approach as the basis for rearing and instructing their charges. As
the advertisement in Wells's *Descriptive Chart* stated: "One of the greatest

difficulties in the training of children arises from not understanding their temperaments and dispositions. This work points out the constitutional differences and how to make the most of each." This particular publication would run you a dollar and a half, presumably because parents had become an easy target for anyone who could convince them that a product was in their children's best interests.

We no longer hear of phrenology. The reason is simple: it has absolutely no validity. The type of localization discussed by its proponents does not exist. The "proof" offered had never come from sound research, but I doubt that there was ever any concern about this shortcoming among its advocates. After all, just consider Wells's area 37C (upper central forehead). Herein lay "the power to discern motives, character, qualities, and physiological conditions." Practitioners, including phrenologists, "have it large."

Having your head examined: the phrenologist's chart.

The Nature-Nurture Controversy

I care to believe that my character flaws, however few, are subject to change, and those who know me well certainly show no desire to discourage me from my goal of self-improvement. But the idea that personality and behavior are governed by scientific laws could mean that change is not possible. I might, for example, discover that one of my flaws was a family tradition that had been passed down through the centuries, courtesy of a defective gene. This might not preclude all hope, but would place considerable restrictions on the extent to which this predisposition could be modified.

Darwin's theory of evolution and Mendel's work on genetics became very influential in the nineteenth century. Some writers interpreted their work as indicating that children were destined to develop in particular ways because of innate characteristics that had been selectively bred into the population. Biological predeterminism had replaced divine will. The way in which these theories were used and interpreted in the childcare literature, however, was often highly biased and sometimes blatantly inaccurate.

Nature in the form of genetically transmitted characteristics was, at one extreme, held to be instrumental in shaping development. Lust, for example, which was supposed to cause all manner of disease and lead ultimately to death, "is transmitted from parent to children as certain as any other element in their nature. This inheritance, however, sometimes skips one generation, but may reappear in the grandchildren or great-grandchildren." Writing in the *Journal of Orificial Surgery,* Doctor E. Miller went on to discuss the heavy onus this placed on parents: "If they are not able or willing to control their sexual desires, the children will not be able to control theirs." This view of genetic mechanisms was far removed from reality. The implication was that one wild night of unbridled passion would warp a gene or two and the parent would become the head of a long line of lustmongers. This ignores the principle that changes occurring through selective breeding typically emerge over a long period of time.

For Dr. Francis Rankin, genetic predeterminism was the biological equivalent of the Biblical references to the sins of the father being visited upon the children for several generations. "How often do we see handsome, stately grandmothers, with clear eyes, fine complexions, erect carriages, and every appearance of good health surrounded by grandchildren of delicate constitutions." At first glance this observation seems more like evidence *against* genetic determinism. Not so. Obviously the grandmother must have erred somewhere along the line and the follies of her "erroneous life" had been passed on to the next generations.

Those representing the nurture side of the controversy argued that environment rather than heredity was the source of the most significant influences on the child. Commenting on the "bad boy," Reverend Goss stated in *Husband, Wife and Home*, "even if a boy is congenitally wrong and has a base heredity, remember the tremendous power of the environment. I for one believe with a growing and increasing faith that the scientists have done the present generation of children an irreparable injury by exaggerating the fateful power of inherited traits. People are hungry for any justification of their neglect of their solemn obligations and it is so easy to excuse our derelictions of duty on the ground of 'heredity.' There needs to be a trumpet sounded in this land to call people back to the old-time sense of parental responsibility."

One consequence of the belief that the environment was instrumental in shaping children's personalities was the emergence of theories concerning critical periods of development. According to some authors, all would have been lost if you had been somewhat preoccupied after delivery and had neglected to pick up the latest book from the childcare section of your local bookstore. Stall declared that "many a mother has been enslaved for life because of the mistakes that she made during the first few weeks after her child was born." The effects of early mismanagement were held to be long term, if not irreversible; the child who did not receive the correct upbringing during the critical period of early development would probably "remain untaught, undisciplined, uncontrolled, and oftentime uncontrollable for the remainder of its childhood and throughout its entire life."

Compromise positions were, of course, possible. Evolution and genetics might lead to certain innate tendencies and limits, but there could also be ample opportunity for the child's experiences to influence how these tendencies would be manifest or where the child would fall within the limits. The interaction of nature and nurture was a recurrent theme in a number of childcare books towards the end of the nineteenth century; what remained in dispute, however, was the relative contribution of each factor.

The nature-nurture controversy is an issue that continues to be debated with passion and sometimes fury. Particularly contentious topics have included whether or not children are born with genetic limitations to their intelligence or predispositions towards antisocial behavior. Gender differences have also been discussed frequently in this context. Are boys more aggressive and competitive because of socialization, or could it be primarily a question of hormonal differences or tendencies that were bred selectively into the male of the species over countless generations? What has changed, however, is the extent to which the need to verify opinions and theories has been recognized. There is nothing intrinsically wrong, for example, in speculating that it is the first few weeks of life or the pattern of bumps on the head that determines the child's future. The Victorian expert, however, expected a type of blind acceptance and faith that has fortunately become harder to secure.

9. The Age of Reason?

TAKING AN HISTORICAL perspective has been a new and totally unexpected experience for me. Until recently, my high school history teacher was remembered only as living proof that the ability to be boring and irrelevant could be a marketable skill. I suspect he sensed our disdain for his subject as he had a habit of delivering a lengthy monologue regarding the importance of studying the past as a means of understanding the present and planning for the future. "Yeah, yeah," we sighed as we shut down the few remaining neurons that had been functioning when the class began and slipped off into our favorite adolescent fantasy.

If I could remember his name I would publicly apologize for my failure to appreciate his wisdom. He was right – I did have an attitude problem, but it was not until I developed an interest in Victorian childcare literature that I achieved this insight. In an effort to demonstrate the sincerity of my apology to my long-suffering teacher, I would like to offer a summary of what I have learned from my excursion into the history of childcare literature.

The Complex Nature of Change

Tuesday was always a special day for my brother and me when we were growing up in Britain. That was the morning our weekly comics were delivered in the newspaper. My choice of which comic to order always distressed my parents; my mother, in particular, wanted me to read something uplifting and she never quite saw the cultural value of Beryll the Peril or the Bash Street Kids. The children in these stories were thoroughly rotten. They had no respect for authority and believed that whims and impulses were to be indulged rather than inhibited. These characteristics instantly endeared them to me: they were my heroes and role models. Unfortunately, the adults in the stories were bound and determined to take all the fun out of life, and in each comic there would be scenes in which Beryll and the other miscreants were being punished. Almost invariably this involved spankings. Beryll's dad seemed to carry a slipper with him at all times, ready to hit his daughter as soon as her latest crime was discovered. The teachers in the stories would also never think of facing the class unless suitably armed – typically with a cane that would be used to deliver "six of the best" on the pupil's backside.

The content of comic strips has changed. Children still misbehave, but parents and teachers do not react with physical punishment. In some parts of the world punishment of this nature has become illegal; where it is still accepted, it can only be used within certain limits. The threshold for defining abuse has been lowered. I can recall certain schoolmasters whose actions would be considered abusive today, but who were operating well within the guidelines of the educational system of their time. The changes that have occurred in attitudes towards discipline have not been isolated, but appear to be just one part of a broader trend. While violence may be increasing in certain areas of society, there has been a growing desire to recognize and curtail its incidence whenever possible.

The Victorian era provides many examples of how this constant process of change in society has far-reaching effects on child-rearing practices. The desire to preserve male dominance in the work force influenced how the role of the mother was portrayed. Similarly, anxiety regarding the declining birth rates in the educated classes helped maintain the view that girls should be groomed only for motherhood. At times the interests were more economic than political. The money that was to be made from infant formula and baby foods created pressure to find and disseminate any information that would support the theory that breast-feeding was not the way to go.

The changes that occurred did not necessarily reflect the self-serving motives of specific interest groups. The industrial revolution, for example, increased the need for education, and it became necessary to question and eventually abandon beliefs that academic instruction could deplete the nerve-force. The concentration of the population in urban areas, and the arrival of motorized transportation systems, made schools more accessible and lessened the need for parents to be directly involved in education. Other factors leading to change were not as noteworthy as the global trends associated with the industrial revolution or the impact of the internal combustion engine; many are probably long-forgotten – such as the effect of the perambulator on infants' daily routines and the extent to which the rubber sheet and washing machine relieved the pressure to complete toilet training as soon as possible.

The criticism of Victorian childcare specialists is not that they were affected by the pressures, developments, and needs of their times, but their apparent failure to recognize that these forces existed. As a result, they tended to present their ideas as absolute truths that might as well be carved in stone.

The sad reality that faces people in my line of work is that we become dated far too quickly and can never hope to realize our dreams of an early retirement supported by an endless stream of royalty cheques. The most we can hope for is that our books will periodically be dusted off the shelves to be included in a historical review of childcare advice.

The Chicken Little Syndrome

I have always wanted to go down in the annals of psychology as someone who was at the leading edge, even if for no more than a fleeting moment. So here is my moment. Freud came up with the Oedipus complex and Jung discovered the collective unconscious; I have discovered the Chicken Little syndrome. At the core of this syndrome is the belief that change is dangerous and has to be viewed with much suspicion, if not fear. From this perspective, the old ways were the best and what might be billed as progress is, in truth, a sign of decay. Those afflicted with the disorder look at society and see sickness; its symptoms are everywhere and must not be ignored.

The Victorian experts had no difficulty finding causes for dismay and alarm. The list of potential problems was very long and ranged from playing cards to bicycles, and homework to bedroom slippers. Children's behavior also provided an abundant supply of material that could be used to fuel people's anxiety. They were spoiled – no longer would a simple stick and hoop satisfy them. The new generation had lost the ability to appreciate what they had, or to work hard for what they did not. They danced (too close and too often), attended far too many parties, and would hop into a sailboat without so much as a second thought. Young people were also victims; they were succumbing to the pressures society had created for them. Candy stores enticed them to sell their souls for a bag of caramels, and novels perverted the minds of young maidens.

The belief that the upcoming generation will, if unchecked, propel the rest of us into oblivion has enjoyed much popularity. "Children today are tyrants, they contradict their parents, gobble their food, and terrorize their teachers." This is a quote that would have appealed to many Victorians; it would also find sympathetic ears today. Its author, however, was Socrates, who took a few moments out of the daily grind of figuring out the meaning of life to comment on the conditions of young people in ancient Greece.

The fact that successive generations have expressed similar concerns about the youth of the day does not, of course, imply that these concerns inevitably lack substance. What I believe is illustrated powerfully by the Victorians, however, is the readiness with which experts can create an atmosphere of doom and gloom and evoke anxiety among parents as a consequence.

Complacency and indifference are not the consequences of a belief in the Chicken Little syndrome. For each generation of parents there will be many issues and risks to be considered and confronted. When our older children were teenagers we watched nervously as they spent more and more time away from home. While we were not worried that they might be sneaking off for clandestine novel-reading sessions or on their way to debauch themselves in a candy store, there were other opportunities to develop habits that could be damaging. Then there was dating. They had survived "wheel-riding," but we worried that they might not be sufficiently prepared to be responsible in their new relationships.

Sometimes the issues facing parents are relatively new, such as the need to take steps to reduce teenage drinking and driving. But I find some comfort in realizing that many of the concerns and questions we have seem almost timeless. With only minor changes to the language and style of writing, much of what is contained in the literature of the last century could be successfully republished today. Discussions regarding such topics such as balancing freedom and discipline, taking care not to "spoil" children, ensuring that the family has time to itself in spite of all the external pressures of work, education, and community activities, and negotiating the respective roles of mothers and fathers, all sound very familiar. Our ancestors struggled with these and many other issues. Their worst fears did not, however, materialize. The fact that they survived makes me optimistic that we will as well; it also encourages me to have a more positive view of the present than is often presented in today's media and child-care literature. The sky has not fallen and I feel no urge to sell all my earthly possessions and perch on top of a mountain waiting for it to do so.

Experts and Consultants

Although the directive "first do no harm" comes from the medical profession, I believe it should be adopted by all those working in the childcare field who are attempting to offer advice that meets the needs of a particular generation of parents. The term expert implies a degree of knowledge and superiority that rarely, if ever, exists. So often Victorians wrote as if they had the absolute truths regarding parenting in their possession. Historians have argued that it is very difficult to be sure that the advice offered was actually followed or even listened to by most parents. Although there may have been many instances in which childcare experts were ignored more than heeded, I would argue that Victorian childcare literature played a role in creating and maintaining attitudes and beliefs that were detrimental to children and families. The myths and taboos surrounding sexuality are a prime example. The fact that extensive and sometimes brutal measures were taken to discourage children from experiencing sexual arousal indicates that a number of parents were convinced that a normal aspect of development was dangerous or even life-threatening. Experts have also convinced mothers not to breast-feed and have dismissed children's complaints of sexual abuse as fantasy. They have attributed autism and schizophrenia to poor mothering and left many parents guilty and angry as a result. They have stated with authority that girls are less intelligent than boys and claimed that young women are physically unsuited to higher education or employment outside the home.

I have to be careful not to sound overly critical of childcare specialists. As a practicing psychologist with a large family and even larger debts, I cannot afford to be unemployed. I am also not as cynical as to believe that all childcare advice is bad. I maintain it can be very valuable, however, for both parents and professionals to look back at the Victorian era and recognize how easy it is for intelligent, educated, and well-meaning people to give and follow advice that is irrelevant, misleading, or harmful.

My recommendation is not to burn all the childcare books and tar and feather their authors. Such a solution would hardly be practical. Ours continues to be a growth industry. It would be possible to spend most of one's professional life traveling to the numerous conferences and seminars that cover every conceivable aspect of children's development and behavior. And there would be no shortage of reading material to help pass the hours spent en route as the number of articles published in scientific journals about childcare has almost tripled over the past two decades. As for the specialized sections of libraries and bookstores, there is every indication that they will continue to grow by leaps and bounds; the list of books in print in North America that have relevance to parenting now exceeds eleven hundred.

As an alternative to banishing the childcare specialists, I would like to suggest a change in job description – from expert to consultant. As a consultant, I believe those of us in the childcare field have a useful purpose to serve. Parents will always have concerns and questions, and there is a role for people whose job is to gather information and ideas through research or during the course of their day-to-day contact with children and families.

No matter how sensible and palatable the reader finds the advice, the "consumer beware" principle will always remain relevant. Consultants may provide up-to-date information, but it is critical to recognize that the vast majority of the research in the field is based on trends. A particular approach may be shown to be effective, but its success rate will never be 100 percent. If the laws that the Victorians discussed as invariant truths actually existed, life would be much simpler; in reality, individual differences are powerful and there will always be children who do not conform to the general trend.

One Last Piece of Advice

As a final comment, I would like to indulge myself. There have been many quotes in this book, but none from myself. I have to admit that I am undoubtedly the only person who is the least bit concerned at this oversight. I would nonetheless like to close with an opinion that I have expressed many times in my lectures, articles and books, and one that I believe applies to most families in most situations. Parents have a unique understanding and appreciation of their children's needs. The daily challenges, rewards, and frustrations of child-rearing provide the experience needed to qualify as the expert – not the number of courses completed or books read. Advice – invited or otherwise – can be of assistance, as was the case in the Victorian times, however, it should be viewed with caution and used only at the parent's discretion.

BIBLIOGRAPHY

Abbott, Jacob. *Gentler Measures in the Management and Training of the Young: The Principles on Which a Firm Parental Authority May be Established and Maintained, Without Violence or Anger, and the Right Development of the Moral and Mental Capacities be Promoted by Methods in Harmony With the Structure and the Characteristics of the Juvenile Mind.* New York: Harper, 1904 (orig. date unknown).

Abbott, Jacob. *The Lucy Books.* New York: Clark, Austin, and Smith, 1841–70.

Abbott, Jacob. *Roldophus.* New York: Harper, 1852.

Abbott, John. *The Mother at Home, or the Principles of Maternal Duty: Familiarly Illustrated.* London, 1834.

Alcott, William. *Gift Book For Young Ladies.* New York: C. M. Saxton (date unknown).

Alcott, William. *The Young Mother or the Physical Education of Children.* Boston: George W. Light, 1836.

Alger, Horatio. *Struggling Upward.* Chicago: M. A. Donohue (date unknown).

Bushnell, Horace. *Views of Christian Nurture and of Subjects Adjacent Thereto.* Hartford: E. Hunt, New York, 1847.

Chavasse, Pye Henry. *Advice to a Wife and Counsel to a Mother.* Philadelphia: J. B. Lippincott, 1984 (orig. c. 1879).

Chesterfield, Philip. *Advice to His Son On the Fine Art of Becoming a Man of the World and a Gentleman.* Washington: M. W. Dunn, 1901.

Cobb, Lyman. *The Evil Tendencies of Corporal Punishment.* New York, 1847.

Edgeworth, Maria. *Moral Tales.* London: Baldwin and Cradock, 1832.

Ellis, Sara. *The Daughters of England: Their Position in Society, Character and Responsibilities.* New York: D. Appleton, 1842.

Fowler, O. S. *Sexual Science*. New York: National Publishing Co., 1870.

Goss, Charles Frederic. *Husband, Wife and Home*. Philadelphia, London and Toronto: Vir Publishing Co., 1897.

Graves, A. J. *Woman in America, Being an Examination Into the Moral and Intellectual Condition of American Female Society*. New York: Harper and Brothers, 1847.

Gregory, John. *A Father's Legacy to His Daughters*. New York: Garland Publishing Co., 1974 (orig. date unknown).

Hardyment, Christina. *Dream Babies: Child Care From Locke to Spock*. Oxford, 1984.

Hoffman, Heinrich. *Struwwelpeter*. London: George Routledge, c. 1909 (orig. date unknown).

Holt, Emmett. *Care and Feeding of Children*. New York and London: D. Appleton and Co., 1943 (orig. c. 1895).

Hood, G. Durant. *The Practical Family Physician*. Chicago: Hood Medical Book Co., 1901.

Kellogg, John. *Plain Facts About Sexual Life*. Michigan: Office of the Health Reformer, 1870.

Kellogg, John. *Plain Facts For Old and Young: Embracing the Natural History and Hygiene of Organic Life*. Iowa: I. F. Segner, Burlington, 1886.

Rankin, Francis. *Hygiene of Childhood: Suggestions For the Care of Children After the Period of Infancy to the Completion of Puberty*. New York: D. Appleton and Co., 1890.

Rousseau, Jean-Jacques. *Emile, or a Treatise on Education*. New York: D. Appleton and Co., 1906 (orig. 1762).

Sigourney, Lydia. *Poems for Their Mothers*. Philadelphia: J. Biddle, 1845.

Stall, Sylvanus. *What a Young Man Should Know*. Philadelphia: Vir Publishing Co., 1897.

Wayland, Francis. *The Elements of Moral Science*. Boston: Gould and Lincoln, 1874.

Wells' New Descriptive Chart For Giving A Delineation of Character According to Phrenology and Physiognomy: For the Use of Practical Phrenologists. London and New York: L. N. Fowler and Co., 1869.

INDEX

ABOUT THE AUTHOR

BORN IN ENGLAND, Dr. Peter Marshall has lived in Canada since 1973. He is the father of five children, and is a child psychologist and a practising clinician in Ontario. His specialized areas of practice are in assertiveness, sexuality, and teenagers. Marshall's previous books include *Cinderella Revisited: How to Survive Your Stepfamily Without a Fairy Godmother* and *Now I Know Why Tigers Eat Their Young: How to Survive Your Teenagers with Humor*, which won a Parents' Choice Award.

PRINTED IN CANADA